POEMS OF
AKHMATOVA

POEMS OF AKHMATOVA

АННА АХМАТОВА

Избранные Стихи

SELECTED, TRANSLATED
AND INTRODUCED
BY
STANLEY KUNITZ
WITH
MAX HAYWARD

A Mariner Book
HOUGHTON MIFFLIN COMPANY
BOSTON · NEW YORK

Quotations from *Hope Against Hope*, by Nadezhda Mandelstam,
copyright © by Atheneum Publishers. English translation,
by Max Hayward, copyright © 1970 by Atheneum Publishers.
Reprinted by permission of the publisher.

For information about this and other Houghton Mifflin trade
and reference books and multimedia products, visit
The Bookstore at Houghton Mifflin on the World Wide Web
at http://www.hmco.com/trade/.

ISBN 0-395-86003-2
CIP DATA IS AVAILABLE.

Printed in the United States of America

QUM 10 9 8 7

Some of these poems originally appeared in *American Poetry Review, Antaeus, Arion's Dolphin, The Atlantic, Hellcoal Annual Two, The Iowa Review, The Nation, New American Review #1* ("Boris Pasternak"), *The New York Review of Books, Partisan Review, Times Literary Supplement, Vogue*. "The Muse," "Lot's Wife," "Epigram," and "The Death of Sophocles" first appeared in *Poetry*.

Содержание

Contents

AKHMATOVA
(1889–1966)

And over the legendary embankment
the real, not the calendar
Twentieth Century drew near.

> — "Poem without a Hero,"
> part I, chapter 3

No foreign sky protected me,
no stranger's wing shielded my face.
I stand as witness to the common lot,
survivor of that time, that place.

> — "Requiem"

ANNA AKHMATOVA was a reticent woman, and even if she had not lived in the extraordinary isolation to which the circumstances of her time condemned her, we would doubtless still know little of her life — except what she chose to say in her verse, and in the brief autobiographical note published in Moscow not long before her death. Reticence was part of her style. It was reflected in her poetry as extreme economy, not to say brusqueness: an imperious take-it-or-leave-it which at once drew attention to her when her work was first published, marking her off from the fashionable poetesses of the day ("poetess" was a word she loathed). Reticence went naturally with the regal manner that caused Marina Tsvetayeva — the only contemporary woman poet she recognized — to call her "Anna Chrysostom of all the Russias." Future biographers will certainly tell much more than she ever let her readers glimpse, but in the meantime enough is known of the bare facts to heighten appreciation of her genius and to suggest the measure of her courage and steadfastness.

Although Akhmatova was born in a suburb of Odessa on the Black Sea, she is indelibly associated with Petersburg and the small town of Tsarskoye Selo ("Tsar's Village"), the imperial summer residence. She was brought to Tsarskoye Selo at the age of one and spent the first sixteen years of her life there. The palace built by Rastrelli, the park, and the Lyceum, founded by Alexander I and attended by Pushkin, are constantly mentioned in her poetry. There could be no more inspiring place for a Russian poet to grow up in. Pushkin was a familiar spirit to her.

"A swarthy youth rambled / by the forlorn lakeshore," she wrote in 1911, and when she returned there in 1944, just before the end of the war, she already had no doubt that she belonged in his company: "Though the branches here are hung with many lyres / a place has been reserved for mine, it seems." In her autobiographical note she recalls it as it was in the nineties, when she was a little girl: "the green, damp magnificence of the parks, the paddock where my nanny took me, the old railway station." The mention of a nanny suggests that her family was comfortably off (her father was a naval engineer), but there was no question of opulence or luxury, and in any case she was notably indifferent to material possessions in later life. Her parents separated in 1905 and her mother took her, with four brothers and sisters, to live in Yevpatoria in the Crimea, where she continued her education at home, after having attended the girls' high school in Tsarskoye Selo. She did her last year of high school in Kiev in 1907 and then went on to the Law Faculty of the Higher Women's Courses there. She enjoyed the history of law and Latin, but soon got bored with the strictly vocational subjects. More important than her formal education was evidently the fact that from an early age her mother read Russian poetry to her: Lermontov, Nekrasov, Derzhavin.

In 1910 she married Nikolai Gumilev. The marriage also marked the beginning of a literary association that proved fateful for her later on.

Gumilev was one of the most colorful figures in Russian poetry before the Revolution. He was the first Russian poet to introduce exotic themes from non-European countries into his work. His travels to Africa (particularly to Abyssinia, in the year after his marriage to Akhmatova) provided material for manly tales and sentiments — there was always, however, an undertone of tragic stoicism and religious awe that lifts his verse above the merely picturesque. His marriage with Akhmatova was not a happy one: many of her poems at that time speak of their wretchedness together ("I Wrung My Hands . . ."), and there is a trenchant sketch of him and their relationship in "Three Things Enchanted Him."

4

Akhmatova got her first taste of Western Europe on honeymoon with Gumilev in Paris, which she visited a second time in the following year (1911). She was impressed by the new boulevards, which were just then being finished off, and by the fact that nobody bought poetry unless it was illustrated by vignettes — poetry, as she puts it, had been "gobbled up" by painting in France. She met Modigliani when he was still poor and unrecognized. They sat in the Jardin du Luxembourg and recited Verlaine to each other. He drew sixteen portraits of her, of which only one survives. She preferred it to any other and kept it hanging in her room to the end of her days. She describes these meetings with Modigliani in a memoir of him published in 1965 and notes with evident nostalgia that the city in which they took place was "vieux Paris et Paris d'avant guerre," where the principal means of transport was still the fiacre. The Russian ballet was all the rage — *The Firebird* was put on in June 1910 — and Chagall had already arrived "with his magical Vitebsk." It must have seemed to her then that Paris could easily have been added to Petersburg as the other pole of her existence. Nothing would have been easier and more natural, in later years, than to take refuge there, as so many of her compatriots did. She stayed in Russia by deliberate choice (as is clear from her poem "I am not one of those who left the land . . . ," 1922), but throughout the years of terror her brief visits to Paris in 1910 and 1911 must have remained in her mind as a fleeting vision of what could have been an alternative to the "cold and darkness of the days to come" which had been foretold by Alexander Blok. She says as much in a poem written in 1944 ("This cruel age has deflected me, / like a river from its course"). In Paris, as she relates in her autobiographical note, she also had her first glimpse of some of the forces preparing "this cruel age": a man called Werner ("a friend of Edison") pointed out two tables in the Taverne du Panthéon: "These are your social democrats — the Bolsheviks here, and the Mensheviks over there."

On her return to Petersburg she began to write verse in a serious way (what she had written earlier, as a schoolgirl, she describes as "feeble"), though her husband was skeptical of her

5

efforts and urged her to go in for the ballet — "you have just the right figure for it," he told her. She was not herself sure what she wanted to do. While Gumilev was away in Abyssinia, she happened to read a proof copy of a posthumous volume of verse, *The Cypress Box*, by Innokenti Annenski, a poet better known as a classical scholar — he taught Greek at the Lyceum in Tsarskoye Selo — and translator of Euripides, Horace, Mallarmé, and Baudelaire, among others. He had died the previous year (1909). Although the Symbolists had claimed him as their own after the appearance of his first volume of verse in 1904, he had very little in common with them. Both in language and themes he was notably "down to earth" and though he could be cryptic, it was the obscurity of extreme precision. Unlike other Symbolists, he had no interest in "other worlds" or in mystical "correspondences" — one recognizes the qualities and temperament that so much appealed to Akhmatova, making Annenski the only avowed modern influence on her. Reading *The Cypress Box* she was, as she records, "oblivious to the world." This sudden illumination was decisive: she had found her voice and what she now wrote impressed even Gumilev on his return from Abyssinia (it was the verse which was to appear in her first collection, *Evening*, published two years later, in 1912). As she makes plain in "To the Muse," she was henceforth wedded only to poetry.

The influence of Annenski was one of the catalysts of change which had been working for some time to hasten the disintegration of Symbolism, the dominating force in Russian letters for well over a decade. Symbolism was more than just a literary school or movement. It was an all-pervading climate of thought, the expression of the Russian Zeitgeist in the years before the historical upheavals ushered in by the First World War. As such, it was also a symptom of the age, a precursor — and some would say an accomplice — of the coming disasters. There were many different strands, often incongruous, or conflicting: end-of-the-century decadence, Nietzscheanism, Christian mysticism (stemming largely from Vladimir Soloviev), and so forth. Geniuses, dabblers, and charlatans were involved side by side in a very diverse and changing movement. The only thing they all

6

recognizably had in common was an urge to escape — from themselves, their society, their culture, the present, their very being — into "other worlds," Christianity, anthroposophy, or paganism, into the past or the future, into cults (of "Beauty," "Art," etc.). It was essentially a romantic impulse, but one that prefigured and anticipated great historical change, instead of following in its wake. The Symbolists believed that the visible here-and-now was illusory and that everything was in any case fated to shatter or decompose — a prospect that filled them with fearful presentiment or longing. Alexander Blok thrilled at the very thought of apocalyptic events. Valeri Bryusov wrote a poem in which he proclaimed his welcome to "the coming Hun." For the Symbolists, poetry was the vehicle of their prophecies, forebodings, and insights into the "beyond." Since things were not what they seemed to be, words were often used as "symbols," instead of in their accepted, everyday senses, and poetry acquired a vatic quality. Some of the leading Symbolists — notably Vyacheslav Ivanov at the famous Wednesday gatherings in his fifth-floor apartment called "the Tower" — behaved almost as high priests. By 1910, however, the movement had lost its cohesion, and in 1912 two dissident groups came out in open revolt against it: the Futurists and the Acmeists. Futurism (of which the best known representatives were Velemir Khlebnikov and Vladimir Mayakovski) was outwardly the more radical and aggressive of the two challenges to Symbolism, advocating contempt for "poetic" language and demanding "autonomy" for the word. Khlebnikov made up his own words, ingeniously forming them from existing roots. In addition to daring neologisms, Mayakovski freely employed the language of the street, to create a provocatively "anti-poetic" effect. Needless to say, the Futurists rejected "mysticism" in all its forms, though Khlebnikov created a fantastic etymological universe of his own, somewhat like Joyce's. Mayakovski, despite the original Futurist demand for autonomy of the word, put his poetry at the service of "protest," both personal and social, and later, after the Revolution, he eagerly lent his gifts to the outright political purpose of propaganda for the new regime. Thus, though it was

7

launched as a movement of emancipation from Symbolism, Futurism was in effect a crude derivative of it: poetry was eventually treated as a means to an end, and, sharing the same romantic impulse, Futurists tended as naturally as Symbolists to become "fellow travelers" of the Revolution.

Acmeism — it was first called this by unfriendly critics — was a more total break with Symbolism. Its three leading exponents — Gumilev, Akhmatova, and Osip Mandelstam — called in question the very attitude to life on which Symbolism was based. The breach came after Vyacheslav Ivanov, at one of his Wednesday gatherings, had denounced a new poem by Gumilev. But this was only the formal pretext. With Mandelstam, Akhmatova, and a few other "dissidents," Gumilev founded a rival group which he called the Poets' Guild. Like Symbolism, Acmeism meant different things to different people — for some it was "classical" precision of language, as opposed to the blurred, polysemantic usage of the Symbolists; to others it implied formal elegance and aestheticism (this was so in the case of Mikhail Kuzmin, who was close to the Acmeists — he wrote a preface to Akhmatova's first volume — though he never joined them); Gumilev seems to have thought of it mainly in terms of a straightforward, narrative style. What they all had in common was a revulsion against the hectic romanticism of the Symbolists, their "ideological" preoccupations and high-priestly pretensions. Most of them believed that language possessed a logic and structure of its own that must not be arbitrarily tampered with (here they differed radically from the Futurists), but treated with the respect a craftsman accords his materials — it was not for nothing that the Acmeists first referred to themselves as Poets' Guild: the word tsekh in Russian can also mean "workshop." Language was like any other material, and in fashioning poetic artifacts from it, one had to take account of its natural qualities and limitations.

It is significant that the leading Acmeists were all fascinated by architecture, in which they plainly saw the best analogy to their view of the poetic function. On her second journey to Paris in 1911, Akhmatova had made a brief trip to northern

8

Italy, visiting Genoa, Florence, Venice and other cities. The impression made on her by Italian painting and architecture, as she says in her autobiographical note, was "enormous" — it was "like a dream you remember all your life." In the twenties, when she could no longer publish original work, her two main preoccupations were Pushkin and the architecture of old St. Petersburg. In 1910, in an important article that was symptomatic of the crisis of Symbolism and presaged the break with it, Kuzmin used architectural imagery to make his point: "I beg you," he said, addressing his fellow poets, "be logical in the design and structure of your work, in syntax . . . be a skillful builder, both in small things and in the whole . . . love words, as Flaubert did, exercise economy in your means, thrift in the use of words, precision and authenticity — then you will discover the secret of a wonderful thing: beautiful clarity." Though this was written before the Acmeists formed into a group, it could well have been their manifesto. Mandelstam, who called his first volume of verse *Stone* (1913), also spoke of poetry in terms of the builder and his materials (as in the quotation below).

But Acmeism — at least for Akhmatova, Gumilev, and Mandelstam — was not only a matter of form, or greater respect for language. This was simply the external aspect of a general attitude or temperament that predisposed them to accept things as they are — not in a complacently conservative sense, but in a spirit of awe and humility before life as it presents itself to the human mind and senses. They thought it almost blasphemy to regard poetry as a means of probing (let alone escaping from) the reality within which man is confined. Gumilev pointed out that the unknowable cannot by definition be known, and Mandelstam considered that knowledge of what is hidden can come only through revelation, not through poetry. At the same time, the Acmeists did not accept the division of the world into "poetic" and "non-poetic" — any experience or perception, however lowly, legitimately came within the poet's sphere. Nadezhda Mandelstam, in her memoir on her husband, *Hope Against Hope,* writes as follows:

The poets and artists who rejected Symbolism do not look down on ordinary, everyday life — on the contrary, it is a source of beauty for them whether they are poets or painters. The Symbolists — such as Vyacheslav Ivanov and Bryusov — assumed the role of high priests standing above everyday life, and for them beauty was something apart from it. By returning to earth, the generation that followed them [i.e., the Acmeists — M. H.] considerably enlarged its horizon, and for it the world was no longer divided into ugly prose and sublime poetry. In this connection I think of Akhmatova, who knew "from what trash poetry, quite unashamed, can grow," and of Pasternak with his passionate defense of the "daily round" in *Dr. Zhivago.* For Mandelstam there was absolutely no problem here: he did not . . . seek to escape into some realm of pure spirit from the earthly confines of our here-and-now. In his essay "The Morning of Acmeism" (1913), he tried to give a poetic justification for remaining attached to the earth with its three dimensions: "The earth is not an encumbrance or an unfortunate accident, but a God-given palace." . . . In the same essay, which was a kind of manifesto, he asked: "What would you think of a guest who, while living at the expense of his host and enjoying his hospitality, actually despises him in his heart of hearts and thinks only of ways to outsmart him?" "Outsmart" here means to escape from time and three-dimensional space. To Mandelstam, as a self-styled Acmeist, three-dimensional space and life on earth were essential because he wanted to do his duty by his "host" — he felt he was here to build, which can only be done in three dimensions. This explains his attitude towards the world of things. In his view, the world was not hostile to the poet or — as he put it — the builder, because things are there to be built from.

This was in essence a religious approach, or at least it implied acceptance of life as a "gift" and the conviction that it could best be lived within a traditional culture from which religion is inseparable. Gumilev and Akhmatova were Russian Orthodox Christians. Mandelstam, a Jew, believed that the highest achievement of human society was in the "Judeo–Christian values" which had first evolved in the Mediterranean world: they constituted the basis of our art and culture. In a remark he made in the thirties, Mandelstam is reported to have defined Acmeism as "nostalgia for world culture." This was said with hindsight, but it probably sums up what the Acmeists were really concerned with before the First World War and the Revolution: namely, to defend Russia's always precarious hold on the essential features of her own culture, which ultimately derived from the same Mediterranean matrix as that of Europe as a whole. The apocalyptically minded Symbolists (and the Futurists *a fortiori*) were in a curious way hypnotized by the Chaos from which this culture had been so arduously won. The thought of its destruction in a holocaust thrilled as much as it may have appalled some of them. Blok, Bely, and Bryusov all to varying degrees believed that by ridding himself in a Dionysian frenzy of the accretions of civilization, man could be mysteriously reborn or transfigured. In the eyes of Akhmatova, Mandelstam, and Gumilev, this was the terrible heresy of the age — just how terrible they were all three to experience with a vengeance. To quote Mandelstam: "One cannot launch a new history — the idea is altogether unthinkable; there would not be the continuity and tradition. Tradition cannot be contrived or learned. In its absence one has, at the best, not history but 'progress' — the mechanical movement of a clock hand, not the sacred succession of interlinked events." It was the aim and effect of the Bolshevik Revolution to put an end to history understood in this way, and to usher in a millennium of "progress." The Acmeists were not "reactionaries" in the sense of opposing social betterment, but they felt that Russia could hardly further her development in any sphere by abandoning the heritage of the previous millennium (in a poem dated 1917, Akhmatova spoke of the country committing "suicide" when "the stern Byzantine spirit abandoned our Russian church"). Neither were they "cosmopolitans." They abhorred the romantic nationalism in the name of which the Symbolists — even Blok — tended to make a virtue out of the self-destructive trait in the Russian character, but they passionately believed in Russia as a rightful heir of the ecumenical values that had been materialized in stone in the churches of Moscow and the architecture of St. Petersburg; it was up to the poet, using the materials of his craft, to "build" in the same spirit.

In October 1912, the same year in which the Poets' Guild was formed and her first book of poetry appeared, Akhmatova's son, Lev, was born. She had no other children.

The moderate success of her first book, followed by acclaim for her second, *Rosary*, two years later, in 1914 (which went through three editions in as many months just before the outbreak of war) established her as a figure of consequence on the literary and social scene of Petersburg. During 1911–1912 she quite frequently read her verse not only at the Poets' Guild, but also at Vyacheslav Ivanov's "Tower" (it was here she first met Mandelstam in 1911). In the autumn of 1913 she found herself together with Blok at a public meeting in honor of the Belgian poet Émile Verhaeren and was asked, to her embarrassment, to read immediately after him. At the end of that year she went to call on Blok to ask him to sign some volumes of his poetry for her. In one he wrote "To Akhmatova — Blok" and into another he copied out a madrigal about her that he had written a couple of weeks earlier. He depicts her in a Spanish shawl with a red rose in her hair — details which, as Akhmatova revealed fifty-two years later in a talk on her meetings with Blok, were completely fictitious. She never became close to him and, for the reasons outlined above, she could not sympathize with a good deal of what he stood for, but he was a figure of enormous importance to her, both as a poet and because he epitomized in his own person the ill-fatedness of the Russian intelligentsia. She later referred to him as "the tragic tenor of the age," and in the culminating work of her life, "Poem without a Hero," he appears as the demonic genius presiding over the ghoulish harlequinade that comes back to her, in 1940, as a nightmare vision of Petersburg society in 1913, the last year of the old era before the beginning of the "real, not the calendar Twentieth Century."

Apart from literary salons and gatherings, there was another place at which the Petersburg intelligentsia met: the celebrated Stray Dog, a *cabaret artistique* opened by Boris Pronin in 1912. Often described in the literary memoirs relating to this period, it consisted of a basement which had been decorated by a leading set designer, Sergei Sudeikin. There was a small stage from which poets of all the contending "schools" came to read their verse to an after-theater crowd: Blok, Bely, Bryusov, Khlebnikov, Mayakovski, Kuzmin, Gumilev, Akhmatova, Yesenin — all appeared here before a larger public than was possible in the more intimate and ingrown literary gatherings. The Stray Dog probably did a good deal to establish the somewhat theatrical element in Russian poetry reading that persists to the present day. The public often went there just for the "show," and it was the scene of many notable encounters. (In her memoir of him, Akhmatova says that Mandelstam introduced her to Mayakovski here; she also relates how Mandelstam once went up to Mayakovski while he was loudly declaiming in his usual stentorian fashion and silenced him by saying: "Mayakovski, stop reading your verse. You are not a Rumanian orchestra.") The atmosphere of the place, the décor, and Akhmatova's feelings at a certain moment about the society for which it was a venue are poignantly evoked in her poem "We're All Drunkards Here . . . ," dated very precisely "1 January 1913." The poem obliquely refers to a tragic event at the very end of 1912 which involved some of the visitors to the Stray Dog and which haunted Akhmatova for decades until, in "Poem without a Hero," it assumed symbolic contours. The actual facts are saved from triteness only by the identity of some of the actors in the drama. A young officer of the dragoons who wrote poetry, Vsevolod Knyazev, was in love with Sudeikin's wife, Olga Glebova-Sudeikina, one of the great beauties of her day, who often appeared in miniature theatrical performances on the stage of the Stray Dog and was a close friend of Akhmatova — they lived together in the same house in Leningrad for several years after the Revolution until Glebova-Sudeikina emigrated to Paris in 1923. On the eve of the New Year, Knyazev shot himself on the stairway of Glebova-

Sudeikina's apartment after discovering that his rival for her affections was Alexander Blok. (This at least is what happened if certain details in "Poem without a Hero" are taken literally — as they are clearly intended to be.) Although the exact circumstances remain obscure, it appears that Akhmatova herself was involved in the affair, sufficiently at any rate to assume some of the burden of guilt, while partly absolving Glebova-Sudeikina (what she felt about her immediately after the event is suggested in the last line of "We're All Drunkards Here..."). But whatever the real facts may have been, they now matter less than the poetic one that this event became, in Akhmatova's eyes, a parable for the sins of a world on which, with the outbreak of war in 1914, a long and terrible retribution began to be exacted.

Akhmatova's second volume of poetry, *Rosary*, is concerned mainly with the intensely personal emotions of this period: the anguish of her unhappy marriage to Gumilev, a gnawing sense of guilt, resignation, and a hint of penitent self-renunciation which perhaps explains the title of the volume. The *amor fati*, already expressed in the first volume in "To the Muse," grows into a conviction that she is above all the embodiment and instrument of her poetic voice. There was nothing of the sibylline affectation of the Symbolists about this, only a matter-of-fact sense of being fated to speak as she does. With her third volume, *White Flock*, which appeared a month or so before the October Revolution, the "pure" lyricism of her early work begins to yield to an epic tone, reflected sometimes in a slightly archaic Derzhavin-like diction; personal experience and memory provide the authority for majestic utterances about things that affected all her compatriots. This tendency reached its climax in the long poems of her later life: "Requiem" and "Poem without a Hero." According to Nadezhda Mandelstam, she became increasingly preoccupied with her "mission" to endure and bear witness. Her own view of her role and situation as a poet under the Soviet regime is obliquely conveyed in such poems as "Dante" (1936), "The Death of Sophocles" and "Alexander at Thebes" (1961).

At the outbreak of the First World War, Gumilev immediately

volunteered for service at the front. Towards the end of the war he was attached to the Russian expeditionary force in France, but he returned home after the October Revolution. This enforced separation led to a final breakdown of the marriage in 1916 and to divorce in 1918. In that same year Akhmatova went to live with an eminent Assyriologist V. K. Shileiko, and during the next two hungry years of the Civil War she earned her meager ration (eking out Shileiko's rather better "academic" one) by working as a librarian at the Institute of Agronomics in Petrograd. Very little is known about her life in these and the subsequent few years. In her memoir of Mandelstam she mentions having met him frequently in 1917–1918, when they sometimes rode in a horse-cab together "over the unbelievable potholes of the Revolutionary winter, among the famous bonfires which were kept alight almost till May, to the crackle of rifle fire coming from Lord knew where." They went together like this several times to the Academy of Arts where they took part in poetry readings for the benefit of the wounded. She also recalls the appearance of the city a little later, in 1920, when she says she lived "in complete isolation," not even seeing Mandelstam: "The Petersburg shop-signs were still there, but behind them was nothing but dust, darkness, and gaping emptiness. It was a time of typhus, famine, shootings, pitch-dark apartments, damp firewood, and people so swollen up as to be unrecognizable. In the Gostiny Dvor you could pick a large bunch of wild flowers. The famous wooden blocks with which the streets of Petersburg had been paved were finally rotting away. You could still smell the chocolate from the basement windows of Kraffts. All the cemeteries had been pillaged. The city had not merely changed, it had turned into the antithesis of itself. But people, particularly the young ones, loved poetry almost as much as they do today" (written in 1965). The demand for poetry, despite the cruel hardships of civil war, was shown by the publication of her third volume, *Plantain*, in 1921.

In the same year Gumilev was shot by the Bolsheviks for his alleged part in a conspiracy, the details of which are still obscure, against the new regime. His execution, which profoundly shocked and frightened the Russian intelligentsia, was a terrible stigma on his ex-wife and son, particularly in the later Stalin years, and also compromised the Acmeists as a group (one of them, Sergei Gorodetski, who had actually founded the Poets' Guild together with Gumilev, only saved his skin by losing no opportunity to revile Gumilev's memory).

A further volume of Akhmatova's verse, *Anno Domini MCMXXI*, incorporating the poems of *Plantain*, came out in 1922, and was followed by a slightly expanded second edition in 1923. After this, scarcely anything more of hers was published in the Soviet Union until 1940. In private conversation many years later she revealed that in 1925, at the height of the "liberal" New Economic Policy, the Central Committee of the Party issued a specific instruction that none of her original work be published. She continued to live in Petersburg, except for a brief period in 1925 when she moved to Tsarskoye Selo. At this time she began to see Mandelstam again and started the close friendship with his wife, Nadezhda, that was to last to the end of her life. In the middle twenties she also left Shileiko for Nikolai Punin, an art historian and critic.

Although she was later to deny rather indignantly the suggestion that she wrote no poetry during the years when she was banned from publication, there is little doubt that in the second half of the twenties and the first half of the thirties, she was affected by the same "dumbness" with which both Mandelstam and Pasternak were stricken at that period. Apart from the Pushkin studies that occupied a good deal of her time in those years (two of her articles on this theme were even published in the thirties), she earned her living by translation, as did many other proscribed or semi-proscribed poets from this time onwards. (Her translation of Rubens's letters appeared in Leningrad in 1933. In later years, particularly after the war, she translated a great deal from numerous languages, working for the most part with the aid of literal versions, including Chinese, Korean, Ancient Egyptian, Bengali, Armenian, Georgian, and Yiddish.) Very few original poems by her are in fact known from these ten "dead" years: they hint at greater despair and

16

bitterness, sufficient in itself to explain her "silence," than she ever voiced in the worse times to come. (In "The Last Toast," for instance, dated 1934: "I drink to our ruined house, / to the dolor of my life, / to our loneliness together . . . / to lying lips that have betrayed us, / to dead-cold, pitiless eyes, / and to the hard realities: / that the world is brutal and coarse, / that God in fact has not saved us.")

There was plenty to be despairing about. Apart from official ostracism, the gathering gloom of Stalinism and her evident personal unhappiness, she suffered constant material hardship and was intermittently ill with tuberculosis. She had lost touch with her family, not that she had ever been very close to them, but their fate can only have increased her distress and loneliness: one brother had been brutally shot during the Civil War, and another committed suicide in the mid-twenties.

In May 1934, she went to stay with the Mandelstams in their Moscow apartment — to raise her return fare to Leningrad she had to sell two objects of sentimental value — and she was there when the secret police came to arrest Mandelstam for his poem denouncing Stalin. In 1935 her son, Lev Gumilev, was arrested during the wave of terror which followed the assassination of Kirov: the name he bore was sufficient reason. In the same year, presumably in the same connection, Nikolai Punin was also arrested. (In "Requiem," the line "At dawn they came and took you away" refers to him. Both were released a year or two later — Punin is known to have been out of prison by 1937, but Lev Gumilev was rearrested in 1938.)

Under the stress of these events, as Stalin's Great Terror began, Akhmatova moved into an intensely creative period, thus bearing out a remark by Mandelstam to the effect that great poetry is often a response to total disaster. Apart from "Requiem" (composed mainly between 1935 and 1940), she wrote a remarkable tribute to Boris Pasternak and the poem called "Voronezh," inspired by her visit in 1936 to Mandelstam, who had been exiled there after Stalin had temporarily reprieved him. (He returned to Moscow in 1937, was again arrested in 1938 and died in a concentration camp near Vladivostok at the end of that year.)

By 1940 Akhmatova's personal circumstances could not have seemed worse. With the Cleopatra of her poem she could say: "Darkness falls, / The trumpets of the Roman eagle scream." In her poem on Mandelstam in Voronezh she had prophesied the horrors of 1937–1938, when Stalin gave his demented Commissar of Internal Affairs seemingly unlimited license to kill and imprison: "in the room of the banished poet / Fear and the Muse stand watch by turn, / and the night is coming on, / which has no hope of dawn."

Miraculously, however — even though her son remained in prison — she benefited from the curious breathing space which the country briefly enjoyed after the abatement of the purges and the signing of Stalin's pact with Hitler in 1939. At the beginning of 1940, a few of Akhmatova's new poems — including the one addressed to Pasternak and "Voronezh" (though, needless to say, without the last four lines quoted above) — were published in two Leningrad literary journals. Even more remarkably, a small selection of her earlier verse, with the addition of some hitherto unpublished items, appeared later in the year under the title *From Six Books*. At this time, too, she appears to have been allowed to join the Union of Soviet Writers — the essential condition for a recognized literary existence.

It is noteworthy that in this same year, when the Soviet Union was for a brief moment peacefully allied with Nazi Germany, Akhmatova's thoughts turned to occupied Paris, and London under bombardment by the Luftwaffe. Perhaps nothing more moving has been written on this theme than "In 1940," which could not of course be published in Russia at the time. This cycle of five poems is an excellent example of her later manner: personal emotions and memories merge with the momentous events of the era and history is refracted, as though in a prism, through the images stirred in her mind by a sudden thought of the past. In 1940 — the end of an era, as she says at the beginning of the first poem — her mind dwelt on an earlier year that had similarly been the last of a whole age: 1913. Thus, London in 1940 was associated in her mind with Petersburg in 1913, and the living link between the two was a friend from that vanished era, Salome Andronnikova (the "beauty of the year '13"), who had left Russia after the Revolution and now lived in London.

An even greater flood of memories about 1913 was unleashed towards the end of 1940. As she subsequently described it herself in a letter to a friend in 1955: "In the autumn of 1940, going through my old papers (which were later destroyed in the Blockade), I came across some letters and poems which I had had for a long time but had not read before. . . . They related to the tragic event of 1913, the story of which is told in 'Poem without a Hero.'" Then, as she records in a prose preface to "Poem without a Hero," she wrote the first part of it, "Petersburg Tale," during one sleepless night on 27 December 1940 — this must have been close to the exact anniversary of Knyazev's suicide. The vision described in the "Poem" evidently came to her that night in her apartment in the old house on the Fontanka canal which had once belonged to the Sheremetyev family and still displayed their coat of arms with the motto *Deus conservat omnia* (Punin had apparently brought her to live here in the mid-twenties).

The "Poem without a Hero" continued to preoccupy her long after its completion in 1943, becoming something of an obsession. As she says in the letter already quoted above: "For fifteen years, again and again, this poem would suddenly come over me, like bouts of an incurable illness (it happened everywhere: listening to music at a concert, in the street, even in my sleep), and I could not tear myself away from it, forever making amendments or additions to a thing that was supposedly finished." Like Lot's wife looking back on her "native Sodom" in her poem of 1925, she looked back "from the year nineteen forty / as from a high tower" and was transfixed by her sudden glimpse of what she had left behind in another era. Why did Knyazev's suicide, of all the events of pre-Revolutionary Petersburg, come back to haunt her so intensely throughout the Second World War and all her own renewed tribulations after it? The episode had seemingly not been uppermost in her mind if this keen recollection of it had been triggered only by the chance discovery

19

of some old papers (the poems she mentions were no doubt Knyazev's, some of them addressed to Glebova-Sudeikina, and published after his death). It was perhaps to be explained in part by a natural inclination to cast around in her mind, as one of the very few of her generation to survive until the "breathing space" of 1940, for something in her own past life to which she could in some way relate the unspeakable calamities that had befallen herself and her contemporaries. It could scarcely have been a question of expecting to find a rational cause, but the thought that these visitations had been *without meaning* would have been intolerable. A woman of her temperament would readily have accepted that the ultimate meaning is hidden and not accessible to human reason, but there is a lesser kind of "meaning" which involves interpretation within a more or less familiar framework. This is often the only way in which the mind can protect itself against insanity (unless one is blessed with the lack of imagination that shields most). It is understandable, therefore, that Akhmatova should have seen the events of her life in terms of sin and expiation: this at least offered the hope and possibility of redemption. It is significant that there are many echoes of Dostoyevski in the "Poem." In the later stages of her work on it, while living in Tashkent in 1942–1943, she spent a good deal of time reading and rereading him, and she must have been profoundly impressed by his reflections on such matters, as well as by his premonitions of the disasters that would flow from unbridled "self-will." There is more than a hint of the "possessed" in the masked revelers — "prattlers and false prophets" — who visit the author on New Year's Eve, 1940, reminding her of the follies that had led, among other things, to the death of a young poet, whom she alone is now left to mourn.

Akhmatova had every reason to know the truth of Pasternak's famous dictum that the overriding sorrows of war, as opposed to the contrived horrors of the purges, came almost as a relief. After the German invasion, when Stalin, on the verge of tears, addressed his subjects over the radio as "brothers and sisters," there was a temporary respite inside the country. Stalin made his peace with the Russian Orthodox Church and, in the face of the threat to Russia's existence, even sought the cooperation of some of his innumerable victims. Akhmatova's son, like many others, was released from imprisonment and sent to serve at the front. In March 1942, *Pravda* published a poem by Akhmatova under the title "Courage." Written in her gravest and most solemn manner, it was no doubt more effective than anything else of its kind to appear at that critical time. Other poems on war themes were written by her during the next two years. In September 1941, as the blockade of Leningrad began, she had spoken over the radio to the women of the city: "The enemy is threatening death and disgrace to the city of Peter, the city of Lenin, of Pushkin, Dostoyevski and Blok." After spending the first winter of the blockade in Leningrad, she was evacuated by plane — clutching the score of Shostakovich's Seventh Symphony — to Tashkent in Central Asia. Here she lived for the next two and a half years in part of an Uzbek-style house, a *balakhana*, which she shared with Mandelstam's widow. A volume of her selected works appeared in 1943 and was immediately sold out. Apart from completing the first draft of the "Poem without a Hero," she wrote some fascinating verse on local themes (such as "Your Lynx-Eyes, Asia . . .").

By the time she returned to Leningrad in June 1944, she had regained some of the public standing she had enjoyed before the Party had deliberately tried to drive her into obscurity. In fact, she had never been forgotten, and her enforced silence of the previous years only served now to heighten her moral authority. For many, indeed, she was quite simply the true voice of Russia. This was demonstrated by an extraordinary and fateful incident in Moscow, in May 1944, where she stayed for a while on her way back to Leningrad from Tashkent. When she appeared at a meeting in the Polytechnic Museum (the largest auditorium in Moscow, where Mayakovski had often declaimed after the Revolution) and read her poetry from the stage, the audience of three thousand people rose to their feet and gave her the sort of ovation normally reserved for the highest in the land. It must have seemed like an act of homage and reconciliation — in the spirit of the eager expectations many Russians now had for a better life after the victory over Germany. But Stalin was already sharpening his knives again. Two years later he is reported (by Zoshchenko) to have asked: "Who organized this standing ovation?"

On her return to Leningrad she was horrified, as she says in her autobiographical note, by "the specter pretending to be my city." She tried to describe her impressions in prose and wrote two pieces which she later destroyed. Her comment on them is worth quoting: "Prose had always seemed to me mysterious and seductive. From the very beginning I had always known about verse, but I had never known anything about prose. Everybody was full of praise for my first experiment, but of course I was skeptical. I called Zoshchenko. He told me to take out a few things and said that he approved of the rest. I was pleased."

At the end of the war she was evidently full of hopes and plans. The publication of a note on them in *Literary Gazette* (the newspaper of the Union of Writers) in November 1945 showed the extent of her "acceptance" into the Soviet literary community. She announced here that at the beginning of the following year the State Publishing House in Leningrad would be bringing out a large volume of her collected works: it was to include all her previous volumes (*Evening, Rosary, White Flock,* etc.), her new wartime poems and a small cycle on Central Asia. She also reported that she was putting together her notes and essays on Pushkin to make a book, and that she was still at work on a long poem, "Triptych," "begun in 1940 and finished in draft form in 1942" (this was in fact "Poem without a Hero," which she continued to rewrite, changing and adding almost to the end of her life.)

But the volume of her poetry never appeared (though it is said to have got as far as being set up in proof, one or two copies of which may have survived). On 14 August 1946, the Central Committee of the Party, with all the stilted formality that was one of the eeriest features of such pronouncements, issued a decree expelling her from the Union of Soviet Writers and forbidding any further publication of her work in the Soviet press. The decree appeared in all the Soviet newspapers and was accompanied by a "report" from Andrei Zhdanov, a member of the Politburo and Stalin's lieutenant in Leningrad. It was the signal for a witches' Sabbath which went on unremittingly till Stalin's death in March 1953. Zhdanov said, in part:

Akhmatova's subject matter is utterly individualistic. The range of her poetry is miserably limited: it is the poetry of an overwrought upper-class lady who frantically races back and forth between boudoir and chapel. She is mainly concerned with amorous-erotic themes which are intertwined with elements of sadness, nostalgia, death, mysticism and doom. . . . A nun or a whore — or rather both a nun and a whore who combines harlotry with prayer . . . Akhmatova's poetry is utterly remote from the people. It is the poetry of the upper ten thousand in old, aristocratic Russia. . . . A Leningrad journal has opened wide its pages to Akhmatova and given her full freedom to poison the minds of our youth with the pernicious spirit of her poetry. . . . What can there be in common between this poetry and the interests of our people and State? Nothing whatsoever. Akhmatova's work belongs to the distant past; it is alien to contemporary Soviet life and cannot be tolerated on the pages of our journals. . . . There is no room in Leningrad for various literary hangers-on and swindlers who want to exploit it for their own purposes. Akhmatova and her like have no time for Soviet Leningrad. They see in it the embodiment of a different social and political order, another ideology."

After accusations of this kind, most people in the Soviet Union would automatically have been arrested in those years. But Stalin had devised a more refined punishment for Akhmatova; though she was henceforth ostentatiously followed by two police agents, she was not otherwise molested. In 1949, however, her son Lev was arrested for a third time. The next day, fearing the kind of delayed search she had witnessed after the arrest of Mandelstam in 1934, Akhmatova burned her papers in the stove of her apartment: a notebook with her verse, the stories mentioned above, and the text of a play she had written in Tashkent. The

23

discovery of this material — particularly the play — would certainly have made her son's position even worse and led to her own arrest as well. The verse — including no doubt "Requiem" — was preserved in her memory and was later written out again without difficulty, but she was unable to reconstitute the original text of the play, which had been in prose. Many years later, toward the end of her life, she wrote some verse fragments as part of a projected new version, but, according to Mrs. Mandelstam, this, even if completed, would have borne little relation to the play actually written in Tashkent in 1942. All that remains is Mrs. Mandelstam's description of it, as performed in front of a few close friends, with Akhmatova playing the leading part in a dress of sackcloth she had designed herself.

The play — or, rather, playlet — was called *Prologue: A Dream within a Dream* and was about the trial of a woman poet before a tribunal of fellow writers, in the presence of representatives of the People. The heroine is never quite sure what she is guilty of; she mumbles pathetic lines of poetry about "a world in which there are air and water, earth and sky, leaves and grass," but her accusers cut her short, saying that nobody has given her the right to mumble verse like this, that she should pause to consider whose mill her verse provided grist for, and that she must answer for it to the People. Those privileged to attend this remarkable performance were reminded of Kafka, Gogol, and Sukhovo-Kobylin (a nineteenth-century Russian playwright who wrote a trilogy about a man trapped in the judicial processes of the bureaucratic state). Akhmatova, on the other hand, thought that she had done no more than compose a perfectly realistic tableau about what had been the actual situation of poets in Russia since the mid-twenties. In this sense the play was not prophetic. But it would have infuriated the police officials dealing with her son's case in 1949.

She had reacted to the Party decree of 1946 and the subsequent campaign of vulgar abuse "without any emotion" (according to Mrs. Mandelstam), but she naturally feared the possible consequences, particularly to her son. The main point in arresting him in 1949 was to use him as a hostage, eventually bringing irresistible pressure to bear on her. The worst punishment Stalin inflicted on poets was not to kill and imprison them, but to make them praise him. This Akhmatova did in 1950, in a series of fifteen poems under the general title "Glory to Peace," published in the weekly illustrated journal *Ogonyok*. They have nothing of Akhmatova in them and were couched in a language which makes it impossible to regard them as anything but a deliberate pastiche of the standard doggerel of the time. One of them, for instance, contains the lines: "And he hears the voice / of his grateful People: 'We have come / to say: Where Stalin is, there is freedom, / Peace and the greatness of our land.'"

Lev Gumilev was released in May 1956, two months or so after the 20th Party Congress at which Khrushchev denounced Stalin in his "secret speech." After this, Akhmatova began to benefit from the process of selective rehabilitation associated with the "Thaw." She was under no illusions about the precarious nature of this improvement in her conditions (in the second half of the fifties she remarked to Mrs. Mandelstam that there are good Caesars and bad Caesars: she was lucky to live to see a good one), but it did mean that she was able to spend her last years in relative serenity, even being allowed a modicum of carefully calculated official recognition. Twenty-two of her poems were republished in an anthology of Soviet poetry which appeared in 1958, and three years later, in 1961, a volume of her verse came out with an afterword by Alexei Surkov, then the secretary of the Union of Writers. Even better, a major new edition of her work, in the preparation of which she had some say, *The Flight of Time*, was published in 1965 with the Modigliani portrait of her on the cover. She was restored to membership in the Union of Writers and at its Congress in 1964 was even elected to the presidium.* In the same year she was allowed to travel abroad for the first time in half a century. The occasion was the award to her of the Etna-Taormina prize in

*This election, one among many others, was purely nominal and honorific, but it has given rise to a misconception that she ended her days as president of the Union of Writers. The idea seems to originate with a misunderstanding based on the use of the word *présidente* in the excellent study of Akhmatova by Jeanne Rude.

Sicily. In her letter of acceptance to Giancarlo Vigorelli, written in Italian, she expressed her joy at receiving this distinction from a country "which I have loved tenderly all my life," particularly as she was about to undertake a translation of Leopardi into Russian and would now have the opportunity "of immersing myself in the Italian language and seeing the house in which the great poet lived and worked." In her autobiographical note she mentions something the thought of which must have given her the greatest pleasure of all, namely that the prize was awarded to her "on the eve of Dante's anniversary."

In June 1965, she was allowed abroad a second time and traveled to England and France. She received the honorary degree of D.Litt., at Oxford, and was able to meet old friends in London and Paris.

When she died the following year on 5 March, it was in the consciousness of having fulfilled her destiny. She could feel that with Osip Mandelstam, Boris Pasternak and Marina Tsvetayeva, she had — in the words of her wartime poem "Courage" — preserved "Russian speech" and kept it "pure and free." It was something she had set out to do when she first joined Mandelstam and Gumilev in the Poets' Guild in 1912. She could scarcely have envisaged how hard the going would be, but she never flinched, and would not have wished her life to be otherwise: ". . . if I could step outside myself / and contemplate the person that I am, / I should know at last what envy is."

— M. H.

St. Antony's College, Oxford

A NOTE ON
THE TRANSLATIONS

PASTERNAK was once rebuked by a pedant who came to his door bearing a long list of the poet's mistakes in translating *Hamlet*. The complaint was greeted with laughter and a shrug: "What difference does it make? Shakespeare and I — we're both geniuses, aren't we?" As if to justify his arrogance, Pasternak's *Hamlet* is today considered one of the glories of Russian literature. Andrei Voznesenski, who passed the anecdote on to me, was unable to recall the visiting critic's name.

The poet as translator lives with a paradox. His work must not read like a translation; conversely, it is not an exercise of the free imagination. One voice enjoins him: "Respect the text!" The other simultaneously pleads with him: "Make it new!" He resembles the citizen in Kafka's aphorism who is fettered to two chains, one attached to earth, the other to heaven. If he heads for earth, his heavenly chain throttles him; if he heads for heaven, his earthly chain pulls him back. And yet, as Kafka says, "all the possibilities are his, and he feels it; more, he actually refuses to account for the deadlock by an error in the original fettering." While academicians insist that poetry is untranslatable, poets continue to produce their translations — never in greater proliferation or diversity than now.

The easiest poets to translate are the odd and flashy ones, particularly those who revel in linguistic display. The translator of Akhmatova, like the translator of Pushkin, is presented with no idiosyncrasy of surface or of syntax to simplify his task. Her poems exist in the purity and exactness of their diction, the authority of their tone, the subtlety of their rhythmic modulations,

29

the integrity of their form. These are inherent elements of the poetry itself, not to be confused with readily imitable "effects." The only way to translate Akhmatova is by writing well. A hard practice!

That is one reason why this volume has been more than five years in preparation. The undertaking began with a feeling of admiration for Akhmatova; it ends with a measure of awe. Her early poems, like those of most young poets, tend to deal with the vicissitudes of love, breathtaking now and then for their dramatic point and reckless candor.

It has been said that Akhmatova derived not so much from other poets as from the great Russian novelists of the nineteenth century. She herself enters into her poems like a character in a work of fiction, or in a play. On New Year's Day, 1913, when she was twenty-three, she broke a poem open with an expostulation that the eventual guardians of the State were to use against her: "We're all drunkards here, and harlots: / how wretched we are together!" On the next New Year's Day she wrote, in bravura novelistic style:

> *"What do you want?" I asked.*
> *"To be with you in hell," he said.*
> *I laughed: "It's plain you mean*
> *to have us both destroyed."*
>
> *He lifted his thin hand*
> *And lightly stroked the flowers:*
> *"Tell me how men kiss you,*
> *tell me how you kiss."*
> — "The Guest," 1914

This was the period of her brilliant, if disastrous, first marriage, when husband and wife were the toast of the Bohemian set of St. Petersburg, he as Gumi-lev (Gumi-lion) and she as Gumi-lvitsa (Gumi-lioness). Her slender grace and aristocratic aquiline profile were as celebrated as her verses. Though in the post-Revolutionary years that followed she was to meet with terrible misfortunes; endure the indignities of poverty, official contempt, and silence; and suffer the death or exile of those dearest to her, she remained proud and spirited. Even in her last days, after her "rehabilitation" — sleazy bureaucratic euphemism! — she refused to wear the geriatric mask of complacence. In delirium she wrote:

> Herewith I solemnly renounce my hoard
> of earthly goods, whatever counts as chattel.
> The genius and guardian angel of this place
> has changed to an old tree-stump in the water.
> — "There Are Four of Us," 1961

Tragedy did not wither her: it crowned her with majesty. Her life, in Keats's phrase, became "a continual allegory," its strands interwoven with the story of a people. Indeed, her poems can be read in sequence as a twentieth-century Russian chronicle. The only way to arrange them is in chronological order.

No poem has been selected for inclusion that was not judged conspicuously fine or representative, either in the body of the work as a whole, or with reference to a specific category, such as the love poems or the "patriotic verse" of World War I. An effort has been made to cover the breadth of Akhmatova's themes and of her expressiveness, which ranges, in Andrei Sinyavski's words, "from a barely audible whisper to fiery oratory, from modestly lowered eyes to thunder and lightning."

I doubt that Akhmatova would have been surprised at the nature of the collaboration responsible for this volume. She herself, as Max Hayward comments in his introduction, translated with outside help from a number of languages, "including Chinese, Korean, Ancient Egyptian, Bengali, Armenian, Georgian, and Yiddish." Translator-poets in the past have consulted linguists as a matter of course, without feeling the need for acknowledging the assistance they received. The modern tendency, reflecting the dynamics of our curiosity about other cultures, is to facilitate and formalize the collaboration between poet and scholar. Largely owing to such combinations of skills, all literatures, however minor or esoteric, are at the point of becoming world literature.

I wish I were a better linguist than I am, but in default of that aptitude I count myself lucky in this partnership. There are plenty of Slavists, but few who can articulate the fine discriminations that mark the language of poetry. For so interdependent an association, the prerequisites are a reciprocity of trust and confidence, together with a congeniality of temperament. On some occasions I have rather boldly rendered a line or a phrase, but always on aesthetic grounds, never because I felt that my information was unreliable. Intuition is a blessing, but it is better to combine it with clarity of understanding.

In certain quarters the literal version of a poem is held sacred, though the term is definitely a misnomer. As Arthur Waley noted: "There are seldom sentences that have word-to-word equivalents in another language. It becomes a question of choosing between various approximations." Translation is a sum of approximations, but not all approximations are equal. Russian word-order, for example, says: "As if I my own sobs / out of another's hands were drinking." One has to rearrange the passage to make it sound idiomatic, and one may even have to sharpen the detail to make it work in English, but one is not at liberty to play arbitrarily with the given. The so-called literal version is already a radical reconstitution of the verbal ingredients of a poem into another linguistic system — at the expense of its secret life, its interconnecting psychic tissue, its complex harmonies. Let me illustrate with a close paraphrase (corrected for word-order) of one of Akhmatova's poems:

> *It's your lynx's eyes, Asia,*
> *that have spied something in me,*
> *have ferreted out something buried,*
> *born of silence,*
> *and fatiguing and difficult,*
> *like midday Termez heat.*
> *As if the whole of proto-memory were flowing*
> *into the mind like molten lava,*

as if I were drinking my own sobs
out of another's hands.

The rendering is conscientious, but the lines are only a shadow of the original text, incapable of producing its singular pleasures. The object is to produce an analogous poem in English out of available signs and sounds, a new poem sprung from the matrix of the old, drenched in memories of its former existence . . . what it said, how it breathed, the inflections of its voice. The Russian poet Nikolai Zabolotski had another figure for the process. He said it was like rebuilding a city out of the evidence of its ruins. To the best of my understanding, the version that follows — like its companions in the collection — is a translation from the Russian, not an adaptation or imitation:

Your lynx-eyes, Asia,
spy on my discontent;
they lure into the light
my buried self,
something the silence spawned,
no more to be endured
than the noon sun in Termez.
Pre-memory floods the mind
like molten lava on the sands . . .
as if I were drinking my own tears
from the cupped palms of a stranger's hands.

Akhmatova is usually described as a formal poet, but in her later years she wrote more and more freely. Some of her poems, particularly the dramatic lyrics that developed out of her histrionic temperament, are so classically joined that they cannot be translated effectively without a considerable reconstruction of their architecture; others are much more fluid in their making. To insist on a universally rigid duplication of metrical or rhyming patterns is arbitrary and pointless, since the effects in any case are not mechanically transferable to another language. Instead of rhyme, our ear is often better pleased by an instrumentation of off-rhyme, assonance, consonance, and other linkages. Prosody is a manifold texture, embodying the expressive range and variety of the human voice. In this connection Osip Mandelstam's widow offers a pertinent commentary:

> In the period when I lived with Akhmatova, I was able to watch her at work as well, but she was much less "open" about it than M., and I was not always even aware that she was "composing." She was, in general, much more withdrawn and reserved than M. and I was always struck by her self-control as a woman—it was almost a kind of asceticism. She did not even allow her lips to move, as M. did so openly, but rather, I think, pressed them tighter as she composed her poems, and her mouth became set in an even sadder way. M. once said to me before I had met Akhmatova —and repeated to me many times afterward—that looking at these lips you could hear her voice, that her poetry was made of it and was inseparable from it. Her contemporaries—he continued—who had heard this voice were richer than future generations who would not be able to hear it.

It may be some comfort to reflect that poets are not easily silenced, even in death. As Akhmatova herself wrote, towards the end, "On paths of air I seem to overhear / two friends, two voices, talking in their turn." Despite the passage of time, the ranks of listeners grow, and the names of Akhmatova and Pasternak and Mandelstam are familiar even on foreign tongues. Some of us are moved to record what we have heard, and to try to give it back in the language that we love.

It would be ungracious to conclude this note without acknowledging our debt to all those who have helped us in the making of this book. We wish to express our gratitude, in particular, to Arthur Gregor, who was the first to encourage us to attempt the translations; to the National Translation Center, Austin, Texas, that expressed its confidence in the undertaking at its very inception by awarding us a generous grant; to the late Manya Harari of London, who made available to us her invaluable notes on "Requiem"; and to Raya Orlova of Moscow, who advised us, with superlative authority, on the selection of poems. We have profited greatly from being able to use the magnificent two-volume edition of Akhmatova's work by Gleb Struve and Boris Filippov, with its wealth of information and comment.

— S. K.

New York

POEMS
OF AKHMATOVA

АННА АХМАТОВА
Избранные Стихи

I.

Читая Гамлета

У кладбища направо пылил пустырь,
А за ним голубела река.
Ты сказал мне: «Ну что ж, иди в монастырь
Или замуж за дурака . . .»

Принцы только такое всегда говорят,
Но я эту запомнила речь, —
Пусть струится она сто веков подряд
Горностаевой мантией с плеч.

— Киев, 1909

I.

Reading Hamlet

A barren patch to the right of the cemetery,
behind it a river flashing blue.
You said: "All right then, get thee to a nunnery,
or go get married to a fool . . ."

It was the sort of thing that princes always say,
but these are words that one remembers.
May they flow a hundred centuries in a row
like an ermine mantle from his shoulders.

— Kiev, 1909

2.

Смуглый отрок бродил по аллеям
У озерных грустил берегов,
И столетие мы лелеем
Еле слышный шелест шагов.

Иглы сосен густо и колко
Устилают низкие пни . . .
Здесь лежала его треуголка
И растрепанный том Парни.

— Царское Село, 1911

2.

Pushkin

A swarthy youth rambled
by the forlorn lakeshore.
A century passes, and we hear
his crackle on the path.

Pine needles, thick, thorny,
bury the stumps of the trees . . .
Here lay his tricorn hat,
his dog-eared verses by Parny.

— Tsarskoye Selo, 1911

3.

Сжала руки под темной вуалью . . .
«Отчего ты сегодня бледна?»
— Оттого, что я терпкой печалью
Напоила его допьяна.

Как забуду? Он вышел, шатаясь,
Искривился мучительно рот . . .
Я сбежала, перил не касаясь,
Я бежала за ним до ворот.

Задыхаясь, я крикнула: «Шутка
Все, что было. Уйдешь, я умру».
Улыбнулся спокойно и жутко
И сказал мне: «Не стой на ветру».

— Киев, 1911

3.

"I Wrung My Hands..."

I wrung my hands under my dark veil . . .
"Why are you pale, what makes you reckless?"
— Because I have made my loved one drunk
with an astringent sadness.

I'll never forget. He went out, reeling;
his mouth was twisted, desolate . . .
I ran downstairs, not touching the banisters,
and followed him as far as the gate.

And shouted, choking: "I meant it all
in fun. Don't leave me, or I'll die of pain."
He smiled at me — oh so calmly, terribly —
and said: "Why don't you get out of the rain?"

— Kiev, 1911

4.

Память о солнце в сердце слабеет.
Желтей трава.
Ветер снежинками ранними веет
Едва-едва.

В узких каналах уже не струится —
Стынет вода.
Здесь никогда ничего не случится, —
О, никогда!

Ива на небе пустом распластала
Веер сквозной.
Может быть лучше, что я не стала
Вашей женой.

Память о солнце в сердце слабеет.
Что это? — Тьма?
Может быть! За ночь прийти успеет
Зима.

— Киев, 1911

4.

"Heart's Memory of Sun..."

Heart's memory of sun grows fainter,
sallow is the grass;
a few flakes toss in the wind
scarcely, scarcely.

The narrow canals no longer flow,
they are frozen over.
Nothing will ever happen here,
oh, never!

In the bleak sky the willow spreads
its bare-boned fan.
Maybe I'm better off as I am,
not as your wife.

Heart's memory of sun grows fainter.
What now? Darkness?
Perhaps! This very night unfolds
the winter.

— Kiev, 1911

5.

Он любил три вещи на свете:
За вечерней пенье, белых павлинов
И стертые карты Америки,
Не любил, когда плачут дети,
Не любил чая с малиной
И женской истерики.
. . . А я была его женой.

— 1911

"Three Things Enchanted Him..."

upper class

Male
Gendered)
   Three things enchanted him:
   white peacocks, evensong,—*evening prayers*
   and faded maps of America.—*adventurous man*

Female
gendered)
   He couldn't stand bawling brats,
   or raspberry jam with his tea,
   or womanish hysteria.
   . . . And he was tied to me.

                             — 1911

A reflection   *hard for divorce*

6.

Музе

Муза-сестра заглянула в лицо,
Взгляд ее ясен и ярок,
И отняла золотое кольцо,
Первый весенний подарок.

Муза! Ты видишь, как счастливы все —
Девушки, женщины, вдовы . . .
Лучше погибну на колесе,
Только не эти оковы.

Знаю: гадая, и мне обрывать
Нежный цветок маргаритку.
Должен на этой земле испытать
Каждый любовную пытку.

Жгу до зари на окошке свечу
И ни о ком не тоскую,
Но не хочу, не хочу, не хочу
Знать, как целуют другую.

Завтра мне скажут, смеясь, зеркала:
«Взор твой не ясен, не ярок . . .»
Тихо отвечу: «Она отняла
Божий подарок».

— Царское Село, 1911

6.

To the Muse

The Muse my sister looked in my face,
her gaze was bright and clear,
and she took away my golden ring,
the gift of the virginal year.

Muse! everyone else is happy —
girls, wives, widows — all around!
I swear I'd rather die on the rack
than live fettered and bound.

In time I'll join the guessing-game,
pluck petals from the daisy's wheel.
Each creature on this earth, I know,
must suffer love's ordeal.

Tonight I pine for no one,
alone in my candlelit room;
but I don't-don't-don't want to know
who's kissing whom.

At dawn the mirrors, mocking, will say:
"Your gaze is not bright or clear."
I'll sigh: "The Muse my sister came
and took the gift of gifts away."

— Tsarskoye Selo, 1911

7.

Все мы бражники здесь, блудницы,
Как невесело вместе нам!
На стенах цветы и птицы
Томятся по облакам.

Ты куришь черную трубку,
Так странен дымок над ней.
Я надела узкую юбку,
Чтоб казаться еще стройней.

Навсегда забиты окошки:
Что там, изморозь иль гроза?
На глаза осторожной кошки
Похожи твои глаза.

О, как сердце мое тоскует!
Не смертного ль часа жду?
А та, что сейчас танцует,
Непременно будет в аду.

— 1 января 1913

7.

"We're All Drunkards Here..."

We're all drunkards here, and harlots:
how wretched we are together!
On the walls, flowers and birds
wait for the <u>clouds to gather.</u>

You puff on your burnished pipe,
strange shapes above you swim,
I have put on a narrow skirt
to show my lines are trim.

The windows are tightly sealed.
What brews? Thunder or sleet?
How well I know your look,
your eyes like a cautious cat.

O heavy heart, how long
before the tolling bell?
But that one dancing there,
will surely rot in hell!

— 1 January 1913

8.

ГОСТЬ

Все, как раньше: в окна столовой
Бьется мелкий метельный снег,
И сама я не стала новой,
А ко мне приходил человек.

Я спросила: «Чего ты хочешь?»
Он сказал: «Быть с тобой в аду».
Я смеялась: «Ах, напророчишь
Нам обоим, пожалуй, беду».

Но поднявши руку сухую,
Он слегка потрогал цветы:
«Расскажи, как тебя целуют,
Расскажи, как целуешь ты».

И глаза, глядевшие тускло,
Не сводил с моего кольца.
Ни один не двинулся мускул
Просветленно-злого лица.

О, я знаю: его отрада —
Напряженно и страстно знать,
Что ему ничего не надо,
Что мне не в чем ему отказать.

— 1 января 1914

8.

The Guest

Nothing is changed: against the dining-room windows
hard grains of whirling snow still beat.
I am what I was,
but a man came to me.

"What do you want?" I asked.
"To be with you in hell," he said.
I laughed, "It's plain you mean
to have us both destroyed."

He lifted his thin hand
and lightly stroked the flowers:
"Tell me how men kiss you,
tell me how you kiss."

His torpid eyes were fixed
unblinking on my ring.
Not a single muscle stirred
in his clear, sardonic face.

Oh, I see: his game is that he knows
intimately, ardently,
there's nothing from me he wants,
I have nothing to refuse.

— 1 January 1914

9.

Александру Блоку

Я пришла к поэту в гости.
Ровно полдень. Воскресенье.
Тихо в комнате просторной,
А за окнами мороз

И малиновое солнце
Над лохматым сизым дымом . . .
Как хозяин молчаливый
Ясно смотрит на меня!

У него глаза такие,
Что запомнить каждый должен;
Мне же лучше, осторожной,
В них и вовсе не глядеть.

Но запомнится беседа,
Дымный полдень, воскресенье
В доме сером и высоком
У морских ворот Невы.

— Январь, 1914

9.

To Alexander Blok

I came to the house of the poet.
Sunday. Precisely at noon.
The room is big and quiet.
Outside, in the frosty view,

hangs a raspberry-colored sun
over ropes of blue-gray smoke.
The gaze of my watchful host
silently envelops me.

His eyes are so serene
one could be lost in them forever.
I know I must take care
not to return his look.

But the talk is what I remember
from that smoky Sunday noon,
in the poet's high gray house
by the sea-gates of the Neva.

— January 1914

10.

Как ты можешь смотреть на Неву,
Как ты можешь всходить на мосты?...
Я недаром печальной слыву
С той поры, как привиделся ты.
Черных ангелов крылья остры,
Скоро будет последний суд,
И малиновые костры,
Словно розы, в снегу цветут.

— 1914

10.

"How Can You Look at the Neva?..."

How can you look at the Neva,
how can you stand on the bridges?...
No wonder people think I grieve:
his image will not let me go.
Black angels' wings can cut one down,
I count the days till Judgment Day.
The streets are stained with lurid fires,
bonfires of roses in the snow.

— 1914

II.

Июль 1914

Пахнет гарью. Четыре недели
Торф сухой по болотам горит.
Даже птицы сегодня не пели,
И осина уже не дрожит.

Стало солнце немилостью Божьей,
Дождик с Пасхи полей не кропил.
Приходил одноногий прохожий
И один на дворе говорил:

«Сроки страшные близятся. Скоро
Станет тесно от свежих могил.
Ждите глада, и труса, и мора,
И затменья небесных светил.

Только нашей земли не разделит
На потеху себе супостат:
Богородица белый расстелет
Над скорбями великими плат».

2

Можжевельника запах сладкий
От горящих лесов летит.
Над ребятами стонут солдатки,
Вдовий плач по деревне звенит.

II.

July 1914

1

All month a smell of burning, of dry peat
smoldering in the bogs.
Even the birds have stopped singing,
the aspen does not tremble.

The god of wrath glares in the sky,
the fields have been parched since Easter.
A one-legged pilgrim stood in the yard
with his mouth full of prophecies:

"Beware of terrible times . . . the earth
opening for a crowd of corpses.
Expect famine, earthquakes, plagues,
and heavens darkened by eclipses.

"But our land will not be divided
by the enemy at his pleasure:
the Mother-of-God will spread
a white shroud over these great sorrows."

2

From the burning woods drifts
the sweet smell of juniper.
Widows grieve over their brood,
the village rings with their lamentation.

Не напрасно молебны служились,
О дожде тосковала земля!
Красной влагой тепло окропились
Затоптанные поля.

Низко, низко небо пустое,
И голос молящего тих:
«Ранят тело твое пресвятое,
Мечут жребий о ризах твоих».

— Слепнево, 20 июля 1914

If the land thirsted, it was not in vain,
nor were the prayers wasted;
for a warm red rain soaks
the trampled fields.

Low, low hangs the empty sky,
tender is the voice of the supplicant:
"They wound Thy most holy body,
They are casting lots for Thy garments."

— Slepnevo, 20 July 1914

12.

Все отнято: и сила, и любовь.
В немилый город брошенное тело
Не радо солнцу. Чувствую, что кровь
Во мне уже совсем похолодела.

Веселой Музы нрав не узнаю:
Она глядит и слова не проронит,
А голову в веночке темном клонит,
Изнеможенная, на грудь мою.

И только совесть с каждым днем страшней
Беснуется: великой хочет дани.
Закрыв лицо, я отвечала ей . . .
Но больше нет ни слез, ни оправданий.

— Севастополь, 24 октября 1916

12.

"All Has Been Taken Away..."

All has been taken away: strength and love.
My body, cast into an unloved city,
is not glad of the sun. I feel my blood
has gone quite cold in me.

I'm baffled by the Muse's state of mind:
she looks at me and doesn't say a word,
and lays her head, in its dark wreath,
exhausted, on my breast.

And only conscience, more terribly each day
rages, demanding vast tribute.
For answer I hide my face in my hands . . .
but I have run out of tears and excuses.

— Sevastopol, 24 October 1916

13.

Мы не умеем прощаться, —
Все бродим плечо к плечу.
Уже начинает смеркаться,
Ты задумчив, а я молчу.

В церковь войдем, увидим
Отпеванье, крестины, брак,
Не взглянув друг на друга, выйдем . . .
Отчего все у нас не так?

Или сядем на снег примятый
На кладбище, легко вздохнем,
И ты палкой чертишь палаты,
Где мы будем всегда вдвоем.

— 1917

13.

"We Don't Know How to Say Goodbye..."

We don't know how to say goodbye:
we wander on, shoulder to shoulder.
Already the sun is going down;
you're moody, I am your shadow.

Let's step inside a church and watch
baptisms, marriages, masses for the dead.
Why are we different from the rest?
Outdoors again, each of us turns his head.

Or else let's sit in the graveyard
on the trampled snow, sighing to each other.
That stick in your hand is tracing mansions
in which we shall always be together.

— 1917

14.

Когда в тоске самоубийства
Народ гостей немецких ждал,
И дух суровый византийства
От русской Церкви отлетал,
Мне голос был. Он звал утешно,
Он говорил: «Иди сюда,
Оставь свой край глухой и грешный,
Оставь Россию навсегда.

Я кровь от рук твоих отмою,
Из сердца выну черный стыд,
Я новым именем покрою
Боль поражений и обид».
Но равнодушно и спокойно
Руками я замкнула слух,
Чтоб этой речью недостойной
Не осквернился скорбный дух.

— 1917

14.

"When in the Throes of Suicide..."

When in the the throes of suicide
our people awaited the German guests,
and the stern Byzantine spirit
abandoned our Russian Church,
I heard a voice — oh it was soothing! —
that cried: "Come here,
leave your wild and sinful country,
leave Russia forever.
I will wash the blood from your hands,
I will pluck the shame from your heart,
I will hide, with a different name,
your insults and your hurts."

But indifferently and calmly
I blocked my ears, like a child,
not to be tempted by dirty talk,
not, in my mourning, to be defiled.

— 1917

15.

Теперь никто не станет слушать песен.
Предсказанные наступили дни.
Моя последняя, мир больше не чудесен,
Не разрывай мне сердца, не звени.

Еще недавно ласточкой свободной
Свершала ты свой утренний полет,
А ныне станешь нищенкой голодной,
Не достучишься у чужих ворот.

— 1917

15.

"Now Nobody Will Want
to Listen to Songs..."

Now nobody will want to listen to songs,
the bitter days foretold come over the hill.
I tell you, song, the world has no more marvels,
do not shatter my heart, learn to be still.

Not long ago, as free as any swallow,
you rode the mornings out, you braved their dangers.
Now you must wander as a hungry beggar,
desperately knocking at the doors of strangers.

— 1917

16.

Чем хуже этот век предшествующих? Разве
Тем, что в чаду печали и тревог
Он к самой черной прикоснулся язве,
Но исцелить ее не мог.

Еще на западе земное солнце светит,
И кровли городов в его лучах блестят,
А здесь уж белая дома крестами метит
И кличет воронов, и вороны летят.

— 1919

"Why Is This Age Worse...?"

Why is this age worse than earlier ages?
In a stupor of grief and dread
have we not fingered the foulest wounds
and left them unhealed by our hands?
In the west the falling light still glows,
and the clustered housetops glitter in the sun,
but here Death is already chalking the doors with crosses,
and calling the ravens, and the ravens are flying in.

— 1919

[handwritten annotations:]
Toppling of Czar, WWI, Revolution, Anarchists...
One war led to another.
- Czar
Cars to disappear individuals.

17.

Все расхищено, предано, продано,
Черной смерти мелькало крыло,
Все голодной тоскою изглодано, —
Отчего же нам стало светло?

Днем дыханьями веет вишневыми
Небывалый под городом лес,
Ночью блещет созвездьями новыми
Глубь прозрачных июльских небес, —

И так близко подходит чудесное
К развалившимся грязным домам . . .
Никому, никому неизвестное,
Но от века желанное нам.

— 1921

17.

"Everything Is Plundered..."

Everything is plundered, betrayed, sold,
Death's great black wing scrapes the air,
Misery gnaws to the bone.
Why then do we not despair?

By day, from the surrounding woods,
cherries blow summer into town;
at night the deep transparent skies
glitter with new galaxies.

And the miraculous comes so close
to the ruined, dirty houses—
something not known to anyone at all,
but wild in our breast for centuries.

— 1921

18.

Не с теми я, кто бросил землю
На растерзание врагам.
Их грубой лести я не внемлю,
Им песен я своих не дам.

Но вечно жалок мне изгнанник,
Как заключенный, как больной.
Темна твоя дорога, странник,
Полынью пахнет хлеб чужой.

А здесь, в глухом чаду пожара
Остаток юности губя,
Мы ни единого удара
Не отклонили от себя.

И знаем, что в оценке поздней
Оправдан будет каждый час . . .
Но в мире нет людей бесслезней,
Надменнее и проще нас.

— 1922

18.

"I Am Not One of Those Who Left the Land..."

I am not one of those who left the land
to the mercy of its enemies.
Their flattery leaves me cold,
my songs are not for them to praise.

But I pity the exile's lot.
Like a felon, like a man half-dead,
dark is your path, wanderer;
wormwood infects your foreign bread.

But here, in the murk of conflagration,
where scarcely a friend is left to know,
we, the survivors, do not flinch
from anything, not from a single blow.

Surely the reckoning will be made
after the passing of this cloud.
We are the people without tears,
straighter than you . . . more proud . . .

— 1922

19.

Лотова жена

И праведник шел за посланником Бога,
Огромный и светлый, по черной горе.
Но громко жене говорила тревога:
Не поздно, ты можешь еще посмотреть

На красные башни родного Содома,
На площадь, где пела, на двор, где пряла,
На окна пустые высокого дома,
Где милому мужу детей родила.

Взглянула, — и, скованы смертною болью,
Глаза ее больше смотреть не могли;
И сделалось тело прозрачною солью,
И быстрые ноги к земле приросли.

Кто женщину эту оплакивать будет?
Не меньшей ли мнится она из утрат?
Лишь сердце мое никогда не забудет
Отдавшую жизнь за единственный взгляд.

— 1922–1924

19.

Lot's Wife

And the just man trailed God's shining agent,
over a black mountain, in his giant track,
while a restless voice kept harrying his woman:
"It's not too late, you can still look back

at the red towers of your native Sodom,
the square where once you sang, the spinning-shed,
at the empty windows set in the tall house
where sons and daughters blessed your marriage-bed."

A single glance: a sudden dart of pain
stitching her eyes before she made a sound . . .
Her body flaked into transparent salt,
and her swift legs rooted to the ground.

Who will grieve for this woman? Does she not seem
too insignificant for our concern?
Yet in my heart I never will deny her,
who suffered death because she chose to turn.

— 1922–1924

20.

Муза

Когда я ночью жду ее прихода,
Жизнь, кажется, висит на волоске.
Что почести, что юность, что свобода
Пред милой гостьей с дудочкой в руке.

И вот вошла. Откинув покрывало,
Внимательно взглянула на меня.
Ей говорю: «Ты ль Данту диктовала
Страницы Ада?» Отвечает: «Я».

— 1924

20.

The Muse

All that I am hangs by a thread tonight
as I wait for her whom no one can command.
Whatever I cherish most — youth, freedom, glory —
fades before her who bears the flute in her hand.

And look! she comes . . . she tosses back her veil,
staring me down, serene and pitiless.
"Are you the one," I ask, "whom Dante heard dictate
the lines of his *Inferno*?" She answers: "Yes."

— 1924

Akhmatova is drawn
to the Inferno

21.

Последний тост

Я пью за разоренный дом,
За злую жизнь мою,
За одиночество вдвоем
И за тебя я пью, —

За ложь меня предавших губ,
За мертвый холод глаз,
За то, что мир жесток и груб,
За то, что Бог не спас.

— 1934

21.

The Last Toast

Her 1st husband was shot, her son self arrested numerous times...

I drink to our ruined house,
to the dolor of my life,
to our loneliness together;
and to you I raise my glass,
to lying lips that have betrayed us,
to dead-cold, pitiless eyes,
and to the hard realities:
that the world is brutal and coarse,
that God in fact has not saved us. — major crisis of faith —
religion was stepped out.

— 1934

81

22.

Борис Пастернак

Он, сам себя сравнивший с конским глазом,
Косится, смотрит, видит, узнает,
И вот уже расплавленным алмазом
Сияют лужи, изнывает лед.

В лиловой мгле покоятся задворки,
Платформа, бревна, листья, облака.
Свист паровоза, хруст арбузной корки,
В душистой лайке робкая рука.

Звенит, гремит, скрежещет, бьет прибоем
И вдруг притихнет, — это значит, он
Пугливо пробирается по хвоям,
Чтоб не спугнуть пространства чуткий сон.

И это значит, он считает зерна
В пустых колосьях, это значит, он
К плите дарьяльской, проклятой и черной,
Опять пришел с каких-то похорон.

И снова жжет московская истома,
Звенит вдали смертельный бубенец . . .
Кто заблудился в двух шагах от дома,
Где снег по пояс и всему конец?

За то, что дым сравнил с Лаокооном,
Кладбищенский воспел чертополох,

22.

Boris Pasternak

He who has compared himself to the eye of a horse
peers, looks, sees, identifies,
and instantly like molten diamonds
puddles shine, ice grieves and liquefies.

In lilac mists the backyards drowse,
and depots, logs, leaves, clouds above;
that hooting train, that crunch of watermelon rind,
that timid hand in a perfumed kid glove . . .

All's ringing, roaring, grinding, breakers' crash —
and silence all at once, release:
it means he is tiptoeing over pine needles,
so as not to startle the light sleep of space.

And it means he is counting the grains
in the blasted ears; it means
he has come again to the Daryal Gorge,
accursed and black, from another funeral.

And again Moscow, where the heart's fever burns.
Far off the deadly sleighbell chimes,
someone is lost two steps from home
in waist-high snow. The worst of times . . .

For spying Laocoön in a puff of smoke,
for making a song out of graveyard thistles,

За то, что мир наполнил новым звоном
В пространстве новом отраженных строф, —

Он награжден каким-то вечным детством,
Той щедростью и зоркостью светил,
И вся земля была его наследством,
А он ее со всеми разделил.

— 19 января 1936

for filling the world with a new sound
of verse reverberating in new space,

he has been rewarded by a kind of eternal childhood,
with the generosity and brilliance of the stars;
the whole of the earth was his to inherit,
and his to share with every human spirit.

— 19 January 1936

23.

Воронеж

О.М.

И город весь стоит оледенелый.
Как под стеклом деревья, стены, снег.
По хрусталям я прохожу несмело.
Узорных санок так неверен бег.
А над Петром воронежским — вороны,
Да тополя, и свод светло-зеленый,
Размытый, мутный, в солнечной пыли,
И Куликовской битвой веют склоны
Могучей, победительной земли.
И тополя, как сдвинутые чаши,
Над нами сразу зазвенят сильней,
Как будто пьют за ликованье наше
На брачном пире тысячи гостей.
А в комнате опального поэта
Дежурят страх и Муза в свой черед,
И ночь идет,
Которая не ведает рассвета.

— 1936

23.

Voronezh

To O.M.

And the town stands locked in ice:
a paperweight of trees, walls, snow.
Gingerly I tread on glass;
the painted sleighs skid in their tracks.
Peter's statue in the square points to
crows and poplars, and a verdigris dome
washed clean, in a cloud of sun-motes.
Here the earth still shakes from the old battle
where the Tatars were beaten to their knees.
Let the poplars raise their chalices
for a sky-shattering toast,
like thousands of wedding guests drinking
in jubilation at a feast.
But in the room of the banished poet
Fear and the Muse stand watch by turn,
and the night is coming on,
which has no hope of dawn.

— 1936

24.

Данте

Он и после смерти не вернулся
В старую Флоренцию свою.
Этот, уходя, не оглянулся,
Этому я эту песнь пою.
Факел, ночь, последнее объятье,
За порогом дикий вопль судьбы.
Он из ада ей послал проклятье
И в раю не мог ее забыть, —
Но босой, в рубахе покаянной,
Со свечей зажженной не прошел
По своей Флоренции желанной,
Вероломной, низкой, долгожданной . . .

— 1936

24.

Dante

Even after his death he did not return
to the city that nursed him.
Going away, this man did not look back.
To him I sing this song.
Torches, night, a last embrace,
outside in her streets the mob howling.
He sent her a curse from hell
and in heaven could not forget her.
But never, in a penitent's shirt,
did he walk barefoot with lighted candle
through his beloved Florence,
perfidious, base, and irremediably home.

— 1936

25.

Подражание армянскому

Я приснюсь тебе черной овцою
На нетвердых, сухих ногах,
Подойду, заблею, завою:
«Сладко ль ужинал, падишах?
Ты вселенную держишь, как бусу,
Светлой волей Аллаха храним . . .
И пришелся ль сынок мой по вкусу
И тебе и деткам твоим?»

— 1930-е гг

25.

Imitation from the Armenian

In the form of a black ewe my ghost
will straggle through your dreams
on faltering, withered legs,
bleating: "Shah of the Shahs,
blessed in Allah's eyes,
how well did you feast?
You hold the world in your hand
as if it were a cold bright bead . . .
But what about my boy,
did you enjoy his taste?"

— In the 30's

26.

Памяти М. Б-ва

Вот это я тебе, взамен могильных роз,
Взамен кадильного куренья;
Ты так сурово жил и до конца донес
Великолепное презренье.
Ты пил вино, ты как никто шутил
И в душных стенах задыхался,
И гостью страшную ты сам к себе впустил

И с ней наедине остался.
И нет тебя, и все вокруг молчит
О скорбной и высокой жизни,
Лишь голос мой, как флейта, прозвучит
И на твоей безмолвной тризне.
О, кто поверить смел, что полоумной мне,
Мне, плакальщице дней погибших,
Мне, тлеющей на медленном огне,
Все потерявшей, всех забывшей, —
Придется поминать того, кто, полный сил,
И светлых замыслов, и воли,
Как будто бы вчера со мною говорил,
Скрывая дрожь предсмертной боли.

— Фонтанный дом, 1940

26.

In Memory of M. B.

Here is my gift, not roses on your grave,
not sticks of burning incense.
You lived aloof, maintaining to the end
your magnificent disdain.
You drank wine, and told the wittiest jokes,
and suffocated inside stifling walls.
Alone you let the terrible stranger in,
and stayed with her alone.

Now you're gone, and nobody says a word
about your troubled and exalted life.
Only my voice, like a flute, will mourn
at your dumb funeral feast.
Oh, who would have dared believe that half-crazed I,
I, sick with grief for the buried past,
I, smoldering on a slow fire,
having lost everything and forgotten all,
would be fated to commemorate a man
so full of strength and will and bright inventions,
who only yesterday, it seems, chatted with me,
hiding the tremor of his mortal pain.

> — The House on the Fontanka, 1940

27.

Клеопатра

I am air and fire . . .
— Shakespeare

Уже целовала Антония мертвые губы,
Уже на коленях пред Августом слезы лила . . .
И предали слуги. Грохочут победные трубы
Под римским орлом, и вечерняя стелется мгла.

И входит последний плененный ее красотою,
Высокий и статный, и шепчет в смятении он:
«Тебя — как рабыню . . . в триумфе пошлет пред собою . . .»
Но шеи лебяжьей все так же спокоен наклон.

А завтра детей закуют. О, как мало осталось
Ей дела на свете — еще с мужиком пошутить
И черную змейку, как будто прощальную жалость,
На смуглую грудь равнодушной рукой положить.

— 1940

27.

Cleopatra

I am air and fire . . .
—Shakespeare

She had already kissed Antony's dead lips,
she had already wept on her knees before Caesar . . .
and her servants have betrayed her. Darkness falls.
The trumpets of the Roman eagle scream.

And in comes the last man to be ravished by her beauty —
such a tall gallant! — with a shamefaced whisper:
"You must walk before him, as a slave, in the triumph."
But the slope of her swan's neck is tranquil as ever.

Tomorrow they'll put her children in chains. Nothing
remains except to tease this fellow out of mind
and put the black snake, like a parting act of pity,
on her dark breast with indifferent hand.

— 1940

28.

Ива

А я росла в узорной тишине,
В прохладной детской молодого века.
И не был мил мне голос человека,
А голос ветра был понятен мне.
Я лопухи любила и крапиву,
Но больше всех серебряную иву.
И, благодарная, она жила
Со мной всю жизнь, плакучими ветвями
Бессонницу овеивала снами.
И — странно! — я ее пережила.
Там пень торчит, чужими голосами
Другие ивы что-то говорят
Под нашими, под теми небесами.
И я молчу . . . Как будто умер брат.

— 1940

28.

Willow

I was raised in checkered silence
in the cool nursery of the young century.
Human voices did not touch me,
it was the wind whose words I heard.
I favored burdocks and nettles,
but dearest to me was the silver willow,
my long companion through the years,
whose weeping branches
fanned my insomnia with dreams.
Oddly, I have survived it:
out there a stump remains. Now other willows
with alien voices intone
under our skies.
And I am silent . . . as though a brother had died.

— 1940

29.

Реквием
1935–1940

Нет, и не под чуждым небосводом,
И не под защитой чуждых крыл, —
Я была тогда с моим народом,
Там, где мой народ, к несчастью, был.

— 1961

ВМЕСТО ПРЕДИСЛОВИЯ

В страшные годы ежовщины я провела семнадцать месяцев в тюремных очередях в Ленинграде. Как-то раз кто-то «опознал» меня. Тогда стоящая за мной женщина с голубыми губами, которая, конечно, никогда не слыхала моего имени, очнулась от свойственного нам всем оцепенения и спросила меня на ухо (там все говорили шепотом):

— А это вы можете описать?

И я сказала:

— Могу.

Тогда что-то вроде улыбки скользнуло по тому, что некогда было ее лицом.

— Ленинград, 1 апреля 1957 года

29.

Requiem
1935–1940

a chant for the peace of the dead, traditionally involving slow sad songs, + prayers.

No foreign sky protected me,
no stranger's wing shielded my face.
I stand as witness to the common lot,
survivor of that time, that place.

— 1961

Impulse to speak for entire country
~like Whitman

INSTEAD OF A PREFACE

p.163

In the terrible years of the Yezhov terror I spent seventeen months waiting in line outside the prison in Leningrad. One day somebody in the crowd identified me. Standing behind me was a woman, with lips blue from the cold, who had, of course, never heard me called by name before. Now she started out of the torpor common to us all and asked me in a whisper (everyone whispered there):

"Can you describe this?"

And I said: "I can."

Role of poet

Then something like a smile passed fleetingly over what had once been her face.

Her face was hardened by misery?

— Leningrad, 1 April 1957

muse of the poem?
Becomes everybody?

Cubism-esque

ПОСВЯЩЕНИЕ

Перед этим горем гнутся горы,
Не течет великая река,
Но крепки тюремные затворы,
А за ними «каторжные норы»
И смертельная тоска.
Для кого-то веет ветер свежий,
Для кого-то нежится закат —
Мы не знаем, мы повсюду те же,
Слышим лишь ключей постылый скрежет
Да шаги тяжелые солдат.
Подымались как к обедне ранней,
По столице одичалой шли,
Там встречались, мертвых бездыханней,
Солнце ниже и Нева туманней,
А надежда все поет вдали.
Приговор . . . И сразу слезы хлынут,
Ото всех уже отделена,
Словно с болью жизнь из сердца вынут,
Словно грубо навзничь опрокинут,
Но идет . . . Шатается . . . Одна . . .
Где теперь невольные подруги
Двух моих осатанелых лет?
Что им чудится в сибирской вьюге,
Что мерещится им в лунном круге?
Им я шлю прощальный свой привет.

— Март 1940

DEDICATION

Such grief might make the mountains stoop,
reverse the waters where they flow,
but cannot burst these ponderous bolts
that block us from the prison cells
crowded with mortal woe. . . .
For some the wind can freshly blow,
for some the sunlight fade at ease,
but we, made partners in our dread,
hear but the grating of the keys,
and heavy-booted soldiers' tread.
As if for early mass, we rose
and each day walked the wilderness,
trudging through silent street and square,
to congregate, less live than dead.
The sun declined, the Neva blurred,
and hope sang always from afar.
Whose sentence is decreed? . . . That moan,
that sudden spurt of woman's tears,
shows one distinguished from the rest,
as if they'd knocked her to the ground
and wrenched the heart out of her breast,
then let her go, reeling, alone.
Where are they now, my nameless friends
from those two years I spent in hell?
What specters mock them now, amid
the fury of Siberian snows,
or in the blighted circle of the moon?
To them I cry, Hail and Farewell!

—March 1940

ВСТУПЛЕНИЕ

Это было, когда улыбался
Только мертвый, спокойствию рад.
И ненужным привеском болтался
Возле тюрем своих Ленинград.
И когда, обезумев от муки,
Шли уже осужденных полки,
И короткую песню разлуки
Паровозные пели гудки.
Звезды смерти стояли над нами,
И безвинная корчилась Русь
Под кровавыми сапогами
И под шинами черных марусь.

1

Уводили тебя на рассвете,
За тобой, как на выносе, шла,
В темной горнице плакали дети,
У божницы свеча оплыла.
На губах твоих холод иконки.
Смертный пот на челе . . . Не забыть! —
Буду я, как стрелецкие женки,
Под кремлевскими башнями выть.

— 1935

2

Тихо льется тихий Дон,
Желтый месяц входит в дом.

P. 163

That was a time when only the dead
could smile, delivered from their wars,
and the sign, the soul, of Leningrad
dangled outside its prison-house;
and the regiments of the condemned,
herded in the railroad-yards,
shrank from the engine's whistle-song
whose burden went, "Away, pariahs!"
The stars of death stood over us.
And Russia, guiltless, beloved, writhed — *the soul of*
under the crunch of bloodstained boots,   *Russia*
under the wheels of Black Marias.

cars.
leaders destroying country.

I

At dawn they came and took you away.   *like a funeral*
You were my dead: I walked behind.
not dead yet In the dark room children cried,
the holy candle gasped for air.   *figure of a saint*
Your lips were chill from the ikon's kiss,   *illegal act, lost rights.*
sweat bloomed on your brow — those deathly flowers!
Like the wives of Peter's troopers in Red Square
I'll stand and howl under the Kremlin towers.

Peter the Great
Loyal troops   — 1935
were executed.

2

Quietly flows the quiet Don;
into my house slips the yellow moon.

Входит в шапке набекрень,
Видит желтый месяц тень.

Эта женщина больна,
Эта женщина одна,

Муж в могиле, сын в тюрьме,
Помолитесь обо мне.

3

Нет, это не я, это кто-то другой страдает.
Я бы так не могла, а то, что случилось,
Пусть черные сукна покроют,
И пусть унесут фонари . . .
       Ночь.

4

Показать бы тебе, насмешнице
И любимице всех друзей,
Царскосельской веселой грешнице,
Что случится с жизнью твоей —
Как трехсотая, с передачею,
Под Крестами будешь стоять
И своей слезою горячею
Новогодний лед прожигать.
Там тюремный тополь качается,
И ни звука — а сколько там
Неповинных жизней кончается . . .

It leaps the sill, with its cap askew,
and balks at a shadow, that yellow moon.

This woman is sick to her marrow-bone,
this woman is utterly alone,

with husband dead, with son away
in jail. Pray for me. Pray.

3

Not, not mine: it's somebody else's wound. *too much suffering for her to bear*
I could never have borne it. So take the thing
that happened, hide it, stick it in the ground.
Whisk the lamps away . . .
        Night.

lamp of awareness

I began w/ dawn

4

innocence before awareness

They should have shown you — mocker,
delight of your friends, hearts' thief,
naughtiest girl of Pushkin's town —
this picture of your fated years,
as under the glowering wall you stand,
shabby, three hundredth in the line, *part of witnessing*
clutching a parcel in your hand,
and the New Year's ice scorched by your tears.
See there the prison poplar bending! *another image of a tree*
No sound. No sound. Yet how many
innocent lives are ending. . . .

105

5

Семнадцать месяцев кричу,
Зову тебя домой.
Кидалась в ноги палачу,
Ты сын и ужас мой.
Все перепуталось навек,
И мне не разобрать
Теперь, кто зверь, кто человек,
И долго ль казни ждать.
И только пыльные цветы,
И звон кадильный, и следы
Куда-то в никуда.
И прямо мне в глаза глядит
И скорой гибелью грозит
Огромная звезда.

6

Легкие летят недели,
Что случилось, не пойму.
Как тебе, сынок, в тюрьму
Ночи белые глядели,
Как они опять глядят
Ястребиным жарким оком,
О твоем кресте высоком
И о смерти говорят.

5

For seventeen months I have cried aloud,
calling you back to your lair.
I hurled myself at the hangman's foot.
You are my son, changed into nightmare.
Confusion occupies the world,
and I am powerless to tell
somebody brute from something human,
or on what day the word spells, "Kill!"
Nothing is left but dusty flowers,
the tinkling thurible, and tracks
that lead to nowhere. Night of stone,
whose bright enormous star
stares me straight in the eyes,
promising death, ah soon!

6

The weeks fly out of mind,
I doubt that it occurred:
how into your prison, child,
the white nights, blazing, stared;
and still, as I draw breath,
they fix their buzzard eyes
on what the high cross shows,
this body of your death.

ПРИГОВОР

И упало каменное слово
На мою еще живую грудь.
Ничего, ведь я была готова,
Справлюсь с этим как-нибудь.

У меня сегодня много дела:
Надо память до конца убить,
Надо, чтоб душа окаменела,
Надо снова научиться жить, —

А не то . . . Горячий шелест лета,
Словно праздник за моим окном.
Я давно предчувствовала этот
Светлый день и опустелый дом.

— Лето, 1939

К СМЕРТИ

Ты все равно придешь — зачем же не теперь?
Я жду тебя — мне очень трудно.
Я потушила свет и отворила дверь
Тебе, такой простой и чудной.
Прими для этого какой угодно вид,
Ворвись отравленным снарядом
Иль с гирькой подкрадись, как опытный бандит,
Иль отрави тифозным чадом.
Иль сказочкой, придуманной тобой
И всем до тошноты знакомой, —

THE SENTENCE   *interrogation*

The word dropped like a stone
on my still living breast.
Confess: I was prepared,
am somehow ready for the test.

So much to do today:
kill memory, kill pain,
turn heart into a stone,
and yet prepare to live again.

Not quite. Hot summer's feast
brings rumors of carouse.
How long have I foreseen
this brilliant day, this empty house?

—Summer, 1939

8.

TO DEATH

You will come in any case — so why not now?
How long I wait and wait. The bad times fall.
I have put out the light and opened the door
for you, because you are simple and magical.
Assume, then, any form that suits your wish,
take aim, and blast at me with poisoned shot,
or strangle me like an efficient mugger,
or else infect me — typhus be my lot —
or spring out of the fairytale you wrote,
the one we're sick of hearing, day and night,

she doesn't fear death — ready for it.

Чтоб я увидела верх шапки голубой
И бледного от страха управдома.
Мне все равно теперь. Клубится Енисей,
Звезда полярная сияет.
И синий блеск возлюбленных очей
Последний ужас застилает.

— Фонтанный Дом, 19 августа 1939

9

Уже безумие крылом
Души закрыло половину,
И поит огненным вином
И манит в черную долину.

И поняла я, что ему
Должна я уступить победу,
Прислушиваясь к своему
Уже как бы чужому бреду.

И не позволит ничего
Оно мне унести с собою
(Как ни упрашивай его
И как ни докучай мольбою):

Ни сына страшные глаза —
Окаменелое страданье, —
Ни день, когда пришла гроза,
Ни час тюремного свиданья,

Ни милую прохладу рук,
Ни лип взволнованные тени,
Ни отдаленный легкий звук —
Слова последних утешений.

— Фонтанный Дом, 4 мая 1940

where the blue hatband *police* marches up the stairs,
led by the janitor, pale with fright.
It's all the same to me. The Yenisei swirls,
the North Star shines, as it will shine forever;
and the blue lustre of my loved one's eyes
is clouded over by the final horror.

— The House on the Fontanka,
19 August 1939

9

Already madness lifts its wing
to cover half my soul.
That taste of opiate wine!
Lure of the dark valley!

Now everything is clear.
I admit my defeat. The tongue
of my ravings in my ear
is the tongue of a stranger.

No use to fall down on my knees
and beg for mercy's sake.
Nothing I counted mine, out of my life,
is mine to take:

not my son's terrible eyes,
not the elaborate stone flower
of grief, not the day of the storm,
not the trial of the visiting hour,

not the dear coolness of his hands,
not the lime trees' agitated shade,
not the thin cricket-sound
of consolation's parting word.

— 4 May 1940

III

РАСПЯТИЕ

«Не рыдай Мене, Мати,
во гробе сущу».

I

Хор ангелов великий час восславил,
И небеса расплавились в огне.
Отцу сказал: «Почто Меня оставил!»
А Матери: «О, не рыдай Мене . . .»

II

Магдалина билась и рыдала,
Ученик любимый каменел,
А туда, где молча Мать стояла,
Так никто взглянуть и не посмел.

— 1940–1943

ЭПИЛОГ

I

Узнала я, как опадают лица,
Как из-под век выглядывает страх,
Как клинописи жесткие страницы
Страдание выводит на щеках,
Как локоны из пепельных и черных
Серебряными делаются вдруг,
Улыбка вянет на губах покорных,
И в сухоньком смешке дрожит испуг.
И я молюсь не о себе одной,

CRUCIFIXION

"Do not weep for me, Mother,
when I am in my grave."

I

A choir of angels glorified the hour,
the vault of heaven was dissolved in fire.
"Father, why hast Thou forsaken me?
Mother, I beg you, do not weep for me. . . ."

II

Mary Magdalene beat her breasts and sobbed,
His dear disciple, stone-faced, stared.
His mother stood apart. No other looked
into her secret eyes. Nobody dared.

comparing herself to Jesus' mother

Her son was in + out of prison — on the front lines.

— 1940–1943

EPILOGUE

I

I have learned how faces fall to bone,
how under the eyelids terror lurks,
how suffering inscribes on cheeks
the hard lines of its cuneiform texts,
how glossy black or ash-fair locks
turn overnight to tarnished silver,
how smiles fade on submissive lips,
and fear quavers in a dry titter.
And I pray not for myself alone . . .

back to woman in preface

113

А обо всех, кто там стоял со мною,
И в лютый холод, и в июльский зной,
Под красною ослепшею стеною.

II

Опять поминальный приблизился час.
Я вижу, я слышу, я чувствую вас:

И ту, что едва до окна довели,
И ту, что родимой не топчет земли,

И ту, что, красивой тряхнув головой,
Сказала: «Сюда прихожу, как домой».

Хотелось бы всех поименно назвать,
Да отняли список, и негде узнать.

Для них соткала я широкий покров
Из бедных, у них же подслушанных слов.

О них вспоминаю всегда и везде,
О них не забуду и в новой беде,

И если зажмут мой измученный рот,
Которым кричит стомильонный народ,

Пусть так же они поминают меня
В канун моего поминального дня.

А если когда-нибудь в этой стране
Воздвигнуть задумают памятник мне,

Согласье на это даю торжество,
Но только с условьем — не ставить его

Ни около моря, где я родилась:
Последняя с морем разорвана связь,

Ни в царском саду у заветного пня,
Где тень безутешная ищет меня,

114

for all who stood outside the jail,
in bitter cold or summer's blaze,
with me under that blind red wall.

[handwritten: Russian Revolution, blood]

II

Remembrance hour returns with the turning year.
I see, I hear, I touch you drawing near:

the one we tried to help to the sentry's booth,
and who no longer walks this precious earth,

and that one who would toss her pretty mane
and say, "It's just like coming home again."

I want to name the names of all that host,
but they snatched up the list, and now it's lost.

I've woven them a garment that's prepared
out of poor words, those that I overheard,

and will hold fast to every word and glance
all of my days, even in new mischance,

and if a gag should blind my tortured mouth,
through which a hundred million people shout,

then let them pray for me, as I do pray
for them, this eve of my remembrance day.

And if my country ever should assent
to casting in my name a monument,

I should be proud to have my memory graced,
but only if the monument be placed

not near the sea on which my eyes first opened —
my last link with the sea has long been broken —

nor in the Tsar's garden near the sacred stump, *[handwritten: willow reference?]*
where a grieved shadow hunts my body's warmth,

115

А здесь, где стояла я триста часов
И где для меня не открыли засов.

Затем, что и в смерти блаженной боюсь
Забыть громыхание черных марусь,

Забыть, как постылая хлопала дверь
И выла старуха, как раненый зверь.

И пусть с неподвижных и бронзовых век
Как слезы струится подтаявший снег,

И голубь тюремный пусть гулит вдали,
И тихо идут по Неве корабли.

— Март 1940

by the prison

but here, where I endured three hundred hours
in line before the implacable iron bars.

Because even in blissful death I fear
to lose the clangor of the Black Marias,

to lose the banging of that odious gate
and the old crone howling like a wounded beast.

And from my motionless bronze-lidded sockets
may the melting snow, like teardrops, slowly trickle,

and a prison dove coo somewhere, over and over,
as the ships sail softly down the flowing Neva.

— March 1940

*She doesn't want to forget
all she's been through...*

117

30.

В сороковом году

Когда погребают эпоху,
Надгробный псалом не звучит,
Крапиве, чертополоху
Украсить ее предстоит.
И только могильщики лихо
Работают. Дело не ждет!
И тихо, так, Господи, тихо,
Что слышно, как время идет.
А после она выплывает,
Как труп на весенней реке, —
Но матери сын не узнает,
И внук отвернется в тоске.
И клонятся головы ниже,
Как маятник, ходит луна.

Так вот — над погибшим Парижем
Такая теперь тишина.

— 1940

30.

In 1940

I

At the burial of an epoch
no psalm is heard at the tomb.
Soon nettles and thistles
will decorate the spot.
The only busy hands are those
of the gravediggers. Faster! Faster!
And it's quiet, Lord, so quiet
you can hear time passing.

Some day it will surface again
like a corpse in a spring river;
but no mother's son will claim her,
and grandsons, sick at heart,
will turn away.
                    Sorrowing heads . . .
The moon swinging like a pendulum . . .

And now, over death-struck Paris,
such silence falls.

2

ЛОНДОНЦАМ

Двадцать четвертую драму Шекспира
Пишет время бесстрастной рукой.
Сами участники грозного пира,
Лучше мы Гамлета, Цезаря, Лира
Будем читать над свинцовой рекой;
Лучше сегодня голубку Джульетту
С пеньем и факелом в гроб провожать,
Лучше заглядывать в окна к Макбету,
Вместе с наемным убийцей дрожать, —
Только не эту, не эту, не эту,
Эту уже мы не в силах читать!

3

ТЕНЬ

Что знает женщина одна о смертном часе?
— О. Мандельштам

Всегда нарядней всех, всех розовей и выше
Зачем всплываешь ты со дна погибших лет
И память хищная передо мной колышет
Прозрачный профиль твой за стеклами карет?
Как спорили тогда — ты ангел или птица!
Соломинкой тебя назвал поэт.
Равно на всех сквозь черные ресницы
Дарьяльских глаз струился нежный свет.
О тень! Прости меня, но ясная погода,
Флобер, бессонница и поздняя сирень
Тебя — красавицу тринадцатого года —

TO THE LONDONERS

Time is now writing with impassive hand
Shakespeare's black play, his twenty-fourth.
What can we do, who know the bitter taste,
but here, by the leaden river, re-enact
those tragic lines of Hamlet, Caesar, Lear? —
or maybe guide, as escort to her tomb,
child Juliet, poor dove, with songs and torches;
or play the Peeping Tom in Macbeth's windows,
trembling no less than the hired murderer.
Only not this one, not this one, not this one —
this one we do not have the strength to read.

3

A SHADOW

What does a certain woman know about the hour of
death?
— O. Mandelstam

You swim up from the past, of all our set
the one most rosy, elegant, and tall.
And your transparent profile — how it sways
through carriage windows! Why does memory insist?
Angel or bird — we argued which you were.
The poet said you were his girl of straw.
Through the black lashes of your Georgian eyes
affection flowed on everyone around.
O shadow! Forgive me, but the clement weather,
Flaubert, insomnia, the smell of lilacs
have turned my thoughts to you, as if that day

И твой безоблачный и равнодушный день
Напомнили . . . А мне такого рода
Воспоминанья не к лицу. О тень!

4

Уж я ль не знала бессонницы
Все пропасти и тропы,
Но эта как топот конницы
Под вой одичалой трубы.
Вхожу в дома опустелые,
В недавний чей-то уют.
Все тихо, лишь тени белые
В чужих зеркалах плывут.
И что там в тумане — Дания,
Нормандия или тут
Сама я бывала ранее,
И это — переиздание
Навек забытых минут?

5

Но я предупреждаю вас,
Что я живу в последний раз.
Ни ласточкой, ни кленом,
Ни тростником и ни звездой,
Ни родниковою водой,
Ни колокольным звоном —
Не буду я людей смущать
И сны чужие навещать
Неутоленным стоном.

— 1940

could bloom again, cloudless and languishing . . .
your day, beauty of the year '13.
But I am troubled by such memories,
O shadow!

4

I know, if anyone does,
the trails and cliffs of insomnia,
but what I did not expect was this cavalry charge
to the blast of a wild trumpet.
Whose are these doors I open?
Somebody's fled from his nest.
How still! how still! Through the mirrors
of strangers white shadows swim.
And that thing shaping there is Denmark — no,
it's Normandy. Or is that ghost myself,
returned to my old haunt,
and this a new edition
of my buried life?

5

But I warn you:
this is my last existence.
Not as swallow, not as maple,
not as reed, or evening-star,
not as water from a spring,
not as bells in a tower,
will I return to vex you,
or walk through strangers' dreams
with stanchless groans.

— 1940

31.

Мужество

Мы знаем, что́ ныне лежит на весах
И что́ совершается ныне.
Час мужества пробил на наших часах.
И мужество нас не покинет.
Не страшно под пулями мертвыми лечь,
Не горько остаться без крова, —
И мы сохраним тебя, русская речь,
Великое русское слово.
Свободным и чистым тебя пронесем,
И внукам дадим, и от плена спасем
            Навеки!

                        — 23 февраля 1942

31.

Courage

We know what trembles on the scales,
and what we must steel ourselves to face.
The bravest hour strikes on our clocks:
may courage not abandon us!
Let bullets kill us — we are not afraid,
nor are we bitter, though our housetops fall.
We will preserve you, Russian speech,
from servitude in foreign chains,
keep you alive, great Russian word,
fit for the songs of our children's children,
pure on their tongues, and free.

— 23 February 1942

32.

Все души милых на высоких звездах.
Как хорошо, что некого терять
И можно плакать. Царскосельский воздух
Был создан, чтобы песни повторять.

У берега серебряная ива
Касается сентябрьских ярких вод.
Из прошлого восставши, молчаливо
Ко мне навстречу тень моя идет.

Здесь столько лир повешено на ветки,
Но и моей как будто место есть.
А этот дождик, солнечный и редкий,
Мне утешенье и благая весть.

— 1944

32.

The Return

The souls of all my dears have flown to the stars.
Thank God there's no one left for me to lose —
so I am free to cry. This air was made
for the echoing of songs.

A silver willow by the shore
trails to the bright September waters.
My shadow, risen from the past,
glides silently towards me.

Though the branches here are hung with many lyres,
a place has been reserved for mine, it seems.
And now this shower, struck by sunlight,
brings me good news, my cup of consolation.

— 1944

33.

Меня, как реку,
Суровая эпоха повернула.
Мне подменили жизнь. В другое русло,
Мимо другого потекла она,
И я своих не знаю берегов.
О, как я много зрелищ пропустила,
И занавес вздымался без меня
И так же падал. Сколько я друзей
Своих ни разу в жизни не встречала.
О, сколько очертаний городов
Из глаз моих могли бы вызвать слезы,
А я один на свете город знаю
И ощупью его во сне найду . . .
И сколько я стихов не написала,
И тайный хор их бродит вкруг меня
И, может быть, еще когда-нибудь
Меня задушит . . .
Мне ведомы начала и концы,
И жизнь после конца, и что-то,
О чем теперь не надо вспоминать.
И женщина какая-то мое
Единственное место заняла,
Мое законнейшее имя носит,
Оставивши мне кличку, из которой
Я сделала, пожалуй, все, что можно.
Я не в свою, увы, могилу лягу . . .

33.

"This Cruel Age Has Deflected Me..."

This cruel age has deflected me,
like a river from its course.
Strayed from its familiar shores,
my changeling life has flowed
into a sister channel.
How many spectacles I've missed:
the curtain rising without me,
and falling too. How many friends
I never had the chance to meet.
Here in the only city I can claim,
where I could sleepwalk and not lose my way,
how many foreign skylines I can dream,
not to be witnessed through my tears.
And how many verses I have failed to write!
Their secret chorus stalks me
close behind. One day, perhaps,
they'll strangle me.
I know beginnings, I know endings too,
and life-in-death, and something else
I'd rather not recall just now.
And a certain woman
has usurped my place
and bears my rightful name,
leaving a nickname for my use,
with which I've done the best I could.
The grave I go to will not be my own.

[Handwritten annotations:]
moment of crisis is so powerful. it causes natural forces to deviate like a parallel life

no control over her life

unwritten verses

she wants to let it out but can't

understated perhaps too horrible to describe?

need for secrecy, alias

she will continue to change

. . . .
Но если бы откуда-то взглянула
Я на свою теперешнюю жизнь,
Узнала бы я зависть наконец . . .

— Ленинград, 1944

But if I could step outside myself
and contemplate the person that I am,
I should know at last what envy is.

— Leningrad, 1944

gesture of liberation

Self recognition of her own talent

sense of gratitude even in the midst of difficulty

34.

Это рысьи глаза твои, Азия,
Что-то высмотрели во мне,
Что-то выдразнили подспудное
И рожденное тишиной,
И томительное, и трудное,
Как полдневный термезский зной.
Словно вся прапамять в сознание
Раскаленной лавой текла,
Словно я свои же рыдания
Из чужих ладоней пила.

— 1945

34.

"Your Lynx-Eyes, Asia..."

Your lynx-eyes, Asia,
spy on my discontent;
they lure into the light
my buried self,
something the silence spawned,
no more to be endured
than the noon sun in Termez.
Pre-memory floods the mind
like molten lava on the sands . . .
as if I were drinking my own tears
from the cupped palms of a stranger's hands.

— 1945

35.

Мартовская элегия

Прошлогодних сокровищ моих
Мне надолго, к несчастию, хватит.
Знаешь сам, половины из них
Злая память никак не истратит:
Набок сбившийся куполок,
Грай вороний и вопль паровоза,
И как будто отбывшая срок
Ковылявшая в поле береза,
И огромных библейских дубов
Полуночная тайная сходка,
И из чьих-то приплывшая снов
И почти затонувшая лодка . . .
Побелив эти пашни чуть-чуть,
Там предзимье уже побродило,
Дали все в непроглядную муть
Ненароком оно превратило.
И казалось, что после конца
Никогда ничего не бывает . . .
Кто же бродит опять у крыльца
И по имени нас окликает?
Кто приник к ледяному стеклу
И рукою, как веткою, машет? . .
А в ответ в паутинном углу
Зайчик солнечный в зеркале пляшет.

— Ленинград, 1960

35.

March Elegy

I have enough treasures from the past
to last me longer than I need, or want.
You know as well as I . . . malevolent memory
won't let go of half of them:
a modest church, with its gold cupola
slightly askew; a harsh chorus
of crows; the whistle of a train;
a birch tree haggard in a field
as if it had just been sprung from jail;
a secret midnight conclave
of monumental Bible-oaks;
and a tiny rowboat that comes drifting out
of somebody's dreams, slowly foundering.
Winter has already loitered here,
lightly powdering these fields,
casting an impenetrable haze
that fills the world as far as the horizon.
I used to think that after we are gone
there's nothing, simply nothing at all.
Then who's that wandering by the porch
again and calling us by name?
Whose face is pressed against the frosted pane?
What hand out there is waving like a branch?
By way of reply, in that cobwebbed corner
a sunstruck tatter dances in the mirror.

— Leningrad, 1960

36.

Эпиграмма

Могла ли Биче словно Дант творить,
Или Лаура жар любви восславить?
Я научила женщин говорить . . .
Но Боже, как их замолчать заставить!

— 1960

36.

Epigram

Could Beatrice have written like Dante,
or Laura have glorified love's pain?
I set the style for women's speech.
God help me shut them up again!

— 1960

37.

Смерть Софокла

На дом Софокла в ночь слетел с небес орел.
И мрачно хор цикад вдруг зазвенел из сада.
А в этот час уже в бессмертье гений шел,
Минуя вражий стан у стен родного града.
Так вот когда царю приснился странный сон:
Сам Дионис ему снять повелел осаду,
Чтоб шумом не мешать обряду похорон
И дать афинянам почтить его отраду.

— 1961

37.

The Death of Sophocles

That night an eagle swooped down from the skies onto
   Sophocles' house.
And the garden suddenly rocked with a cry of cicadas.
Already the genius strode toward his immortality,
skirting the enemy camp at the walls of his native city.
Then it was that the king had a strange dream:
Great Dionysus ordered him to lift the siege,
so as not to dishonor the service for the dead
and to grant the Athenians the solace of his fame.

— 1961

38.

Александр у Фив

Наверно, страшен был и грозен юный царь,
Когда он произнес: «Ты уничтожишь Фивы».
И старый вождь узрел тот город горделивый,
Каким он знал его еще когда-то встарь.

Все, все предать огню! И царь перечислял
И башни, и врата, и храмы — чудо света,
Но вдруг задумался и, просветлев, сказал:
«Ты только присмотри, чтоб цел был Дом Поэта».

— Ленинград, октябрь 1961

38.

Alexander at Thebes

The young king must have been terrible to behold
commanding his captain: "You will destroy Thebes,"
while the city loomed in the old soldier's sight,
storied and proud, as he remembered it.

Put it all to the torch! And the king named one by one
the towers, the gates, the temples — this marvel of the world;
then brightened, as the thought leaped into words:
"Only be sure the Poet's House is spared."

— Leningrad, October 1961

39.

Нас четверо

...И отступилась я здесь от всего,
От земного всякого блага,
Духом — хранителем «места сего»
Стала лесная коряга.

Все мы немного у жизни в гостях,
Жить — это только привычка,
Слышится мне на воздушных путях
Двух голосов перекличка.

Двух...а еще у восточной стены,
В зарослях крепкой малины,
Свежая темная ветвь бузины
Словно — письмо от Марины.

— в Гавани, ноябрь 1961
(в бреду)

39.

There Are Four of Us

Herewith I solemnly renounce my hoard
of earthly goods, whatever counts as chattel.
The genius and guardian angel of this place
has changed to an old tree-stump in the water.

Earth takes us in awhile as transient guests;
we live by habit, which we must unlearn.
On paths of air I seem to overhear
two friends, two voices, talking in their turn.

Did I say two? . . . There by the eastern wall,
where criss-cross shoots of brambles trail,
— O look! — that fresh dark elderberry branch
is like a letter from Marina in the mail.

— November 1961
(in delirium)

40.

Из Поэмы без героя

ИЗ ГОДА СОРОКОВОГО,
КАК С БАШНИ, НА ВСЕ ГЛЯЖУ.
КАК БУДТО ПРОЩАЮСЬ СНОВА
С ТЕМ, С ЧЕМ ДАВНО ПРОСТИЛАСЬ,
КАК БУДТО ПЕРЕКРЕСТИЛАСЬ
И ПОД ТЕМНЫЕ СВОДЫ СХОЖУ.

Осажденный Ленинград,
25 августа 1941 г.

Новогодний вечер. Фонтанный Дом. К автору, вместо того, кого ждали, приходят тени тринадцатого года под видом ряженых. Белый зеркальный зал. Лирическое отступление — «Гость из Будущего». Маскарад. Поэт. Призрак.

Я зажгла заветные свечи,
   Чтобы этот светился вечер,
      И с тобой, ко мне не пришедшим,
         Сорок первый встречаю год.
Но . . .
      Господняя сила с нами!
      В хрустале утонуло пламя
         «И вино, как отрава, жжет».

40.

From Poem without a Hero

FROM THE YEAR NINETEEN FORTY
AS FROM A HIGH TOWER I LEAN,
  ONCE MORE BIDDING GOODBYE
  TO WHAT I LONG AGO FORSOOK,
AS THOUGH I HAVE CROSSED MYSELF
AND AM GOING DOWN UNDER DARK
VAULTS.

crossing present
& past
&
Religious
crossing

> — Leningrad under siege,
> 25 August 1941

New Year's Eve. The House on the Fontanka. Instead of the person she was expecting, the author is visited by shadows from the year 1913 disguised as mummers. A white hall of mirrors. Lyrical digression: "A Visitor from the Future." Masquerade. A poet. A ghost.

I have lit my treasured candles,
one by one, to hallow this night.
With you, who do not come,
I wait the birth of the year.
Dear God!
          the flame has drowned in crystal,
and the wine, like poison, burns.
Old malice bites the air,

Это всплески жесткой беседы,
    Когда все воскресают бреды,
        А часы все еще не бьют . . .
Нету меры моей тревоге,
    Я сама, как тень на пороге,
        Стерегу последний уют.
И я слышу звонок протяжный,
    И я чувствую холод влажный,
        Каменею, стыну, горю . . .
И, как будто припомнив что-то,
    Повернувшись вполоборота,
        Тихим голосом говорю:
«Вы ошиблись: Венеция дожей —
    Это рядом . . . Но маски в прихожей,
        И плащи, и жезлы, и венцы
Вам сегодня придется оставить.
Вас я вздумала нынче прославить,
    Новогодние сорванцы!»
Этот Фаустом, тот Дон-Жуаном,
    Дапертутто, Иоканааном;
        Самый скромный — северным Гланом
        Иль убийцею Дорианом,
            И все шепчут своим Дианам
            Твердо выученный урок.
                А какой-то еще с тимпаном
                Козлоногую приволок.
И для них расступились стены,
    Вспыхнул свет, завыли сирены,
        И, как купол, вспух потолок.
Я не то что боюсь огласки . . .
    Чтò мне Гамлетовы подвязки!
        Чтò мне вихрь Саломеиной пляски,
        Чтò мне поступь Железной Маски!
            Я сама пожелезней тех . . .
И чья очередь испугаться,
    Отшатнуться, отпрянуть, сдаться
        И замаливать давний грех ? . .

old ravings rave again,
though the hour has not yet struck.
Dread. Bottomless dread . . .
I am that shadow on the threshold
defending my remnant peace.
The insistent doorbell rings.
My marrow's chilled.
I turn to stone, ice, fire . . .
and, as though struck by memory,
half-turning round,
I say in a far-off voice:
"You've come to the wrong place,
the Doges' Palace is next door,
but welcome! Leave in the hall
your masks, cloaks, scepters, crowns.
My pleasure is to celebrate you now,
New Year's revelers!
Here's one who comes as Faust,
and there's Don Juan,
John the Baptist, Dapertutto,
and, modestly, the Nordic Glahn,
or maybe Dorian Gray, the murderer,
all whispering glib confections
into the ears of their Dianas.
And then there's one man with a drum
trailed by a goatlegged nymph.
For them the walls have parted,
lights cascade, sirens wail,
and the ceiling swells like a cupola.
Let the gossip roll!
What to me are Hamlet's garters,
or the whirlwind of Salome's dance,
or the tread of the Man in the Iron Mask?
I am more iron than they.
Whose turn is it now to be afraid —
to recoil, back away, yield,
ask pardon for an ancient sin?

Ясно все:

      не ко мне, так к кому же!

Не для них здесь готовился ужин,

И не им со мной по пути.

Хвост запрятал под фалды фрака . . .

    Как он хром и изящен . . .

                  Однако . . .

    Я надеюсь, Владыку Мрака

      Вы не смели сюда ввести? . .

Маска это, череп, лицо ли —

    Выражение злобной боли,

      Что лишь Гойя смел передать.

Общий баловень и насмешник, —

    Перед ним самый смрадный грешник —

      Воплощенная благодать . . .

Веселиться — так веселиться! —

    Только как же могло случиться,

      Что одна я из них жива?

Завтра утро меня разбудит,

    И никто меня не осудит,

      И в лицо мне смеяться будет

        Заоконная синева.

Но мне страшно: войду сама я,

    Кружевную шаль не снимая,

      Улыбнусь всем и замолчу.

С той, какою была когда-то,

    В ожерельи черных агатов,

      До долины Иосафата

        Снова встретиться не хочу . . .

Не последние ль близки сроки? . . .

    Я забыла ваши уроки,

      Краснобаи и лжепророки,

        Но меня не забыли вы.

Как в прошедшем грядущее зреет,

    Так в грядущем прошлое тлеет —

      Страшный праздник мертвой листвы.

Clearly it's me
they seek, cocoon of souls,
though not my kind; and not
for them was supper prepared.
But look! there's one who hides his tail
under his frock. His limp is elegant.
Surely you have not dared to bring
The Prince of Darkness here.
What is it? Mask or skull or face?
Goya alone could limn
that rictus of dolor and of rage.
Prince Charming, prince of the mockers —
compared with him the foulest of sinners
is grace incarnate . . .
Enough! On with the fun!
But why, among them, must I be
the only one alive?
Tomorrow morning I shall wake
and nobody will accuse me.
Through the window the bluest sky
will laugh in my face. But now
I am afraid. I shall present myself,
not taking off my lace shawl,
and manage a vague smile
before falling silent.
That woman I once was,
in a black agate necklace,
I do not wish to meet again
till the Day of Judgment.
Are the last days near, perhaps?
I have forgotten your lessons,
prattlers and false prophets,
but you haven't forgotten me.
As the future ripens in the past,
so the past rots in the future —
a terrible festival of dead leaves.

Б
Е
Л
Ы
Й

З
А
Л

Звук шагов тех, которых нету,
По сияющему паркету,
И сигары синий дымок.
И во всех зеркалах отразился
Человек, что не появился
И проникнуть в тот зал не мог.
Он не лучше других и не хуже,
Но не веет Летейской стужей,
И в руке его теплота.
Гость из Будущего! — Неужели
Он придет ко мне в самом деле,
Повернув налево с моста?

... С детства ряженых я боялась,
Мне всегда почему-то казалось,
Что какая-то лишняя тень
Среди них «без лица и названья»
Затесалась ...

Откроем собранье
В новогодний торжественный день!
Ту полночную Гофманиану
Разглашать я по свету не стану
И других бы просила ...

Постой,
Ты как будто не значишься в списках,
В калиострах, магах, лизисках,
Полосатой наряжен верстой, —
Размалеван пестро и грубо —
Ты ...

ровесник Мамврийского дуба,
Вековой собеседник луны.
Не обманут притворные стоны,
Ты железные пишешь законы;
Хаммураби, ликурги, солоны
У тебя поучиться должны.
Существо это странного нрава,
Он не ждет, чтоб подагра и слава

A sound of steps of those not here
over the gleaming parquet floor,
and the blue smoke of a cigar.
All the mirrors on the wall
show a man not yet appeared
who could not enter this white hall.
He is no better and no worse,
but he is free of Lethe's curso:
his warm hand makes a human pledge.
Strayed from the future, can it be
that he will really come to me,
turning left from the bridge?

From childhood I have been afraid
of mummers. It always seemed
an extra shadow
without face or name
had slipped among them . . .
On this ceremonial eve
let us begin by calling the roll.
And may others respect
the reticence I feel
about my midnight Tale of Hoffmann.
But wait!
            your name is not to be listed
with the others, not with
Cagliostros, Magi, Messalinas;
you come in the gaudy stripes
of a painted milepost;
you . . .
            who are as old as the Mamre oak,
ancient interrogator of the moon,
whose feigned groans cannot take us in.
You write laws of iron.
Hammurabi, Lycurgus, Solon
could take lessons from you.
Creature of special tastes,

Впопыхах усадили его
В юбилейные пышные кресла,
А несет по цветущему вереску
По пустыням свое торжество.
И ни в чем не повинен: ни в этом
Ни в другом и ни в третьем . . .
                        Поэтам
Вообще не пристали грехи.
Проплясать пред Ковчегом Завета
Или сгинуть! . .
                 Да что там! Про это
Лучше их рассказали стихи.
Крик петуший нам только снится,
За окошком Нева дымится,
Ночь бездонна и длится, длится —
Петербургская чертовня . . .
В узких окнах звезды не видно,
Гибель где-то здесь, очевидно,
Но бездумна, легка, бесстыдна
Маскарадная болтовня . . .
Крик:
    «Героя на авансцену!»
Не волнуйтесь: дылде на смену
Непременно выйдет сейчас
И споет о священной мести . . .
Что ж вы все убегаете вместе,
Словно каждый нашел по невесте,
Оставляя с глазу на глаз
Меня в сумраке с черной рамой,
Из которой глядит тот самый,
Ставший наигорчайшей драмой
И еще не оплаканный час.

Это все наплывает не сразу,
Как одну музыкальную фразу,
Слышу шепот: «Прощай! Пора!

you do not wait for gout and fame
to elevate you
to a luxurious jubilee chair,
but bear your triumph
over the flowering heather,
over wildernesses.
And you are guilty of nothing: neither of this,
that, nor anything . . .
                    Besides,
what have poets, in any case, to do with sin?
They must dance before the Ark of the Covenant
or die! But what am I trying to say?
Their own verses spell it out.
We only dream the cock's crow,
the Neva smokes beyond the window,
the night is fathomless, and it goes on and on —
this Petersburg bacchanalia.
In the black sky no star is seen,
somewhere in ambush lurks the Angel of Death,
but the spiced tongues of the masqueraders
are loose and shameless.
A shout:
                    "Make way for the hero!"
Ah yes. Displacing the tall one,
he will step forth now without fail
and sing to us about holy vengeance . . .
But why are you all running away,
as if each of you had found a bride,
leaving me face to face
in the gloom with a black picture-frame,
out of which stares that very hour,
prologue to the bitterest drama of my life,
which I have yet to expiate.

Slowly it floods my mind
like a musical phrase.
"Goodbye!" I hear him whisper.

Я оставлю тебя живою,
Но ты будешь моей вдовою,
Ты — Голубка, солнце, сестра!»
На площадке две слитые тени...
После — лестницы плоской ступени,
Вопль: «Не надо!» и в отдаленьи
Чистый голос:
                    «Я к смерти готов».

Факелы гаснут, потолок опускается. Белый (зеркальный) зал снова делается комнатой автора. Слова из мрака:

Смерти нет — это всем известно,
    Повторять это стало пресно,
        А что есть — пусть расскажут мне.
Кто стучится?
                Ведь всех впустили.
Это гость зазеркальный. Или
    То, что вдруг мелькнуло в окне...
Шутки ль месяца молодого,
    Или вправду там кто-то снова
        Между печкой и шкафом стоит?
Бледен лоб, и глаза открыты...
    Значит, хрупки могильные плиты,
        Значит, мягче воска гранит...
Вздор, вздор, вздор! — От такого вздора
    Я седою сделаюсь скоро
        Или стану совсем другой.
Что ты манишь меня рукою?!

За одну минуту покоя
Я посмертный отдам покой.

"I shall leave you behind.
but you will be my widow.
O my dove, my star, my sister!"
On the landing two locked shadows . . .
then the broad steps plunge beneath.
"Don't do it!" In the distance
a pure voice: "I am ready for death."

The torches go out, the ceiling drops into place. The white
hall of mirrors becomes the author's room. Words from the
darkness:

There is no death, each of us knows —
it's banal to say.
I'll leave it to others to explain.
That knocking!
               I thought all of them were here.
Is this the visitor from the wrong side
              of the mirror? Or the shape
that suddenly flitted past my window?
Is it the new moon playing tricks,
or is someone really standing there again
between the stove and the cupboard?
Pale forehead. Open eyes . . .
This means that gravestones are fragile
and granite is softer than wax.
Absurd, absurd, absurd! From such absurdity
I shall soon turn gray
or change into another person.
Why do you beckon me with your hand?

        For one moment of peace
        I would give the peace of the tomb.

NOTES
ON THE POEMS

No ATTEMPT will be made here to deal with the complicated textology of Akhmatova's poems. Such matters are exhaustively treated in the only full and scholarly edition of her work: *Anna Akhmatova: Sochinenia*, in two volumes, edited by G. P. Struve and B. A. Filippov (Inter-Language Literary Associates, second edition, revised and enlarged, 1967–1968). It should be noted that in the successive editions of her work, Akhmatova often added to earlier cycles poems that had in fact been published much later. "Reading Hamlet," for example, was first published in a Leningrad journal only in 1946 and was subsequently included in the cycle bearing the title of her first published volume, *Evening (Vecher,* 1912), to which it chronologically and thematically belongs.

Poems 1–6: From *Evening.* All except "Pushkin" and "To the Muse" refer to Nikolai Gumilev, whom Akhmatova first met as a schoolgirl in Tsarskoye Selo.

Mandelstam once pointed out that Akhmatova owes much to the tradition of the nineteenth-century Russian realist novel: a series of short lyrics, taken together, constitute a narrative, with snatches of dialogue, telling incidents or details. This is certainly the hallmark of her early manner, and is well illustrated here.

2 "Pushkin": Evariste Parny (1753–1814) was a French writer of neoclassical amatory verses.

4 "Heart's Memory of Sun . . .": "In the bleak sky the willow spreads / its bare-boned fan." Lines like this have led some critics to see Far Eastern influence — via Art Nouveau — in Akhmatova's early poetry (see, for example, the fascinating article by Alexis Rannit, "Anna Akhmatova Considered in the Context of Art Nouveau," in volume 2 of the Struve-Filippov edition). Whether or not there was influence, there was apparently some affinity. In 1956 she published a volume of translations of Korean classical poetry, to which she felt drawn because, as she said, "it is close to painting."

Evening exhibits occasional other mannerisms (such as the "ermine mantle" in the first poem) suggesting the influence of Mikhail Kuzmin, who wrote a preface to the volume when it first appeared. Such slightly coy traces of stylization are completely absent from Akhmatova's second volume, *Rosary*.

Poems 7–9: From *Rosary* (*Chetki,* 1914).

7 "We're All Drunkards Here . . .": When it was first published in the journal *Apollon* in 1913, this poem was titled "Cabaret Artistique" (see Introduction, pp. 13–14).

Poems 10–13: From *White Flock* (*Belaya staya,* 1917). Most of the poems in this volume were written during the years of the First World War and the early days of the Revolution.

10 "How Can You Look at the Neva? . . .: "the streets are stained with lurid fires, / bonfires of roses in the snow." This line, referring to the bonfires which were customarily lit in the streets of Petersburg during the winter to melt the snow, indicates that the poem was written months before the war.

11 "July 1914": Slepnevo was the country estate belonging to Akhmatova's mother-in-law, where she spent her summers after her marriage to Gumilev.

12 "All Has Been Taken Away . . .": "My body, cast into an unloved city." Akhmatova knew Sevastopol from her childhood days, when her family spent summer holidays there. In 1916 she separated from Gumilev (they were divorced two years later).

Poems 14-19: From *Plantain (Podorozhnik),* and *Anno Domini,* both published in 1921 (second edition in 1923). Most of the poems here were written during the period of the Revolution and Civil War.

14 "When in the Throes of Suicide . . .": In all the later Soviet editions of Akhmatova's work, the first four lines of this poem are omitted.

15 "Now Nobody Will Want to Listen to Songs . . .": In the latest Soviet edition of Akhmatova's poetry, *The Flight of Time (Beg Vremeni,* 1965), the date of this poem has been deliberately changed to "1916" by the editors, so that it does not appear to relate to the Revolution.

19 "Lot's Wife": One of three poems about women in the Old Testament (the other two were Rachel and Michal). This is one of the most celebrated and quoted of Akhmatova's poems.

Poems 20-24 and 27-28: From *Reed (Trostnik),* the name which Akhmatova gave to a selection of poems published for the first time in 1940, though many had been written much earlier. With this volume she was allowed to break her long "silence" since 1924. Other poems, written during the years of the Second World War, were later added to *Reed.*

20 "The Muse": This is one of five poems that Akhmatova at various times addressed to the Muse. She read and could recite Dante in the original.

22 "Boris Pasternak": The Daryal Gorge runs through the Caucasus into Georgia, which Pasternak often visited in the thirties to see his friends, the poets Paolo Yashvili and Titsian Tabidze. (Both perished in the purges, a year after this poem was written.)

23 "Voronezh": Voronezh is a historical city situated on a tributary of the Don about three hundred miles to the south of Moscow. Peter the Great built a flotilla there for his conquest of Azov, near the mouth of the Don. The site of the battle of Kulikovo (1380), at which Dmitri Donskoi beat the Tatars, is not far away. Osip Mandelstam (the "O. M." of the dedication) lived there in exile from 1934 to 1937. Akhmatova's visit to him in 1936, after which she wrote this poem, is described in Nadezhda Mandelstam's *Hope Against Hope*. The poem was originally published in 1940 without the last four lines, and was printed in full in the Soviet Union only in *The Flight of Time*.

Poem 25 "Imitation from the Armenian": This poem was published for the first time in the Soviet magazine *Radio and Television*, in 1966. The vagueness of the dating ("the '30's") is no doubt intentional since, despite the "Armenian" disguise, the poem clearly refers to the arrest of Akhmatova's son, Lev Gumilev. It could thus have been written either in 1935 or in 1938.

Poem 26 "In Memory of M. B.": First published in *Poetry Day* (*Den poezii*), Leningrad, 1966. Mikhail Bulgakov (1891–1940), to whose memory the poem is addressed, was an outstanding novelist, satirist, and playwright, most of whose work was banned in the last years of his life, and after his death well into the post-Stalin era. A physician by training, he knew in advance that he was about to die — i.e., he had "let the terrible stranger in." His most remarkable novel, *The Master and Margarita*, completed in the last year of his life, was not published in the Soviet Union till 1966.

Poem 29 "Requiem": The full text of this lament for the victims of Stalin's terror was first published abroad (in Munich, 1963). A few excerpts have been published in the Soviet Union, but without any indication that they belong to a larger whole. The three stanzas of section 7 were published as long ago as 1940 in the literary journal *Zvezda* (one of the two Leningrad journals closed on Party orders in 1946, after the denunciation of

Akhmatova), but without the title, "The Sentence." The four lines of section 3 were published in a Moscow literary journal in 1966. The section entitled "Crucifixion" appeared in *The Flight of Time* in 1965. The various parts of the main text were written between 1935 and 1940, but the verse and prose prefaces were added in 1961 and 1957 respectively.

"Instead of a Preface": "Yezhov terror" (*yezhovshchina*), the name often given by Russians to the worst period of the purges (1937–1938) when Nikolai Yezhov, the Commissar of Internal Affairs, was ordered by Stalin to proceed to indiscriminate mass arrests. People waited outside the prisons in the hope of learning something about the fate of their relatives, or of getting a parcel to them.

Section 1: "At dawn they came and took you away." As Akhmatova mentions in her memoir on Mandelstam, this line refers specifically to the arrest of Nikolai Punin in 1935, before the Yezhov terror began. By then, according to a reference in the second volume of Mrs. Mandelstam's memoirs, Punin was at liberty again, and appears not to have been rearrested, unlike Akhmatova's son.

"Peter's troopers": *Streltsy*, household troops founded by Ivan the Terrible. After their mutiny in 1698, they were crushed by Peter the Great's Scottish general, Patrick Gordon, and two thousand of them were put to death after torture. Their wives pleaded for them "under the Kremlin walls."

Section 2: "With husband dead" refers to Nikolai Gumilev, shot in 1921. These four couplets are a good example of Akhmatova's occasional use of very simple rhythms and diction, close to those of folk poetry. Despite her high literary culture, she had a strong affinity to this style and was very fond, for example, of the verse of the nineteenth-century populist Nekrasov. It appealed to the deeply "peasant" side of her nature once noted by Mandelstam. The diction here expresses her sense of the universality of the national tragedy.

Section 4: "Pushkin's town": Tsarskoye Selo in the original Russian.

"Under the glowering wall": The original here names the notorious Leningrad political prison Kresty (literally "Crosses," because of the shape of the internal layout), possibly with some intentional allusion to the literal meaning.

Section 8: "To Death": "Where the blue hatband marches up the stairs": members of the internal security forces (NKVD) wear blue hatbands.

Poem 30 "In 1940": The various parts of this cycle were all published at different times in the Soviet Union — "At the Burial of an Epoch" in 1946, "To the Londoners" in 1943, "A Shadow" in 1960, "I Know, if Anyone Does" in 1944 and "But I Warn You" in 1945.

"A Shadow" refers to Salome Andronnikova, "the beauty of the year '13," who still lives in London. She is of Georgian origin. Mandelstam addressed a famous poem to her in 1916, in which he made a pun on her name, turning "Salome" into the Russian diminutive *solominka,* meaning literally "little straw." (There is an image in Mandelstam's poem about drinking through a straw.) The epigraph to "A Shadow" is from another poem by Mandelstam addressed to a certain Olga Vaksel, who emigrated to Norway in the twenties and committed suicide there. The last seven lines of "I Know, if Anyone Does" are evidently an exact description of the genesis of "Poem without a Hero."

Poem 32 "The Return": First published in 1945, this poem is about Akhmatova's return to Leningrad and Tsarskoye Selo from Tashkent, via Moscow, in 1944.

"This air was made. . . ." The original has "The air of Tsarskoye Selo" — the name has been left out in translation here and elsewhere because of its phonetic awkwardness in English.

Poem 33 "This Cruel Age Has Deflected Me . . .": First published in 1964, this is the third in a series of four "Northern Elegies" which are to some extent thematically connected with "Poem without a Hero." The first of the "Elegies," entitled

"Prehistory," is a brilliant evocation of the Russia of Dostoyevski ("the convict of Omsk") and a superbly ironical comment on the fate of those destined to be born, like Akhmatova's generation, around the time of his death: "The country was delirious and the convict of Omsk / Had understood it all and shown it up for what it was . . . / Just then we decided to be born / and, judging the time exactly right / if we were not to miss a single moment of spectacles / never seen before, we took our leave of non-being." Akhmatova here, as in "Poem without a Hero," expresses the wonderment of many of her contemporaries at having been born on the threshold of an era which was to witness "spectacles" of such unreality that it was impossible not to brood on the illusoriness of time itself and even the coordinates of one's own identity. There is nothing mystical about this: it was dictated by the stark actualities of "that time, that place," and the feeling Akhmatova so vividly conveys in the present poem was familiar to Dostoyevski, as it was to Kafka (whose work Akhmatova knew and appreciated).

Poem 34 "Your Lynx-Eyes, Asia . . .": First published in *Novy Mir* in 1965 and the last of a cycle of a dozen or so poems about Central Asia (mostly written in Tashkent during 1942–1944) to which Akhmatova subsequently gave the general title "The Moon at Its Zenith." These poems are marked by an awed sense of timelessness, even of déjà vu, which is also one of the themes of "Poem without a Hero." She described Central Asia as "the motherland of motherlands," saying in one of the poems: "I have not been here for seven hundred years, / But nothing has changed . . . / God's grace flows in the same way / From irrefutable mountaintops." Another of these poems begins: "Have I become someone else / from what I was there, by the sea? / Have my lips forgotten your taste, O sorrow? / In this old parched land / I am home again, / A Chinese wind sings in the haze, / And all is familiar."

Termez: a town on the Soviet-Afghan frontier.

Poem 35   "March Elegy": Published in the year it was written, in a Moscow literary journal.

Poem 36   "Epigram": Written and published in 1960.

Poem 39   "There Are Four of Us. . . .": The full text was first published in a New York Russian literary almanac, *Vozdushnye puti* (*Paths of Air* — by coincidence the poem contains the same phrase, which is an allusion to the title of a story by Pasternak written in 1925). In this version it is entitled "There Are Four of Us" and has epigraphs from poems addressed to Akhmatova by all three poets alluded to in the text: Mandelstam, Pasternak, and Tsvetayeva. In the version published in *The Flight of Time*, the title is "Komarovo Sketches," and there is only one epigraph from Marina Tsvetayeva — "O Muse of weeping," the first line of a poem to Akhmatova written in 1916.

Komarovo, to which the poem refers, is about fifty miles from Leningrad on the Karelian isthmus. During the last years of her life Akhmatova had a dacha there. It was given to her by the Union of Writers — one of the rare favors bestowed on her after her "rehabilitation." She is buried there.

Poem 40   "Poem without a Hero": The full text of "Poem without a Hero: A Triptych" was first published in the New York Russian literary almanac *Vozdushnye puti* in 1960, and although many extracts from it have appeared in the Soviet Union, it has still not been published there in its entirety. The present volume contains only the first chapter of the poem's Part One, which is called "The Year Nineteen Hundred and Thirteen: A Petersburg Tale." (We have also omitted the preface and three dedications in verse, including one to Knyazev and another to Glebova-Sudeikina.) The three further chapters of Part One continue with a detailed portrait of the "heroine," Olga Glebova-Sudeikina, a description of Petersburg in 1913, and a dramatic account of the young poet's suicide after he has seen Glebova-Sudeikina return home from a performance at the

Stray Dog, accompanied by someone "without face or name."
Part Two (which is preceded by an epigraph in English, "My
future is in my past" — said to have been the motto of Mary
Queen of Scots) opens with a kind of scherzo in which there is a
conversation with an imaginary editor in the Soviet present. He
is disconcerted by the confusion of Part One: "You can't make
out who's dead and who survived, / who the author is and who
the hero, / or why today we need such / gossip about a poet and
this swarm of ghosts." The author explains that she was not
herself glad of "this infernal harlequinade" and would have
preferred it to pass her by — the visitation had come because
"the devil made me rummage in a trunk." She hints at the
connection between the ghosts of the past and the fate of her
generation: "And we could tell you, / how we lived beside
ourselves with fear, / how we reared our children for the
executioner, / the torture chamber and the prison cell." Part
Two ends with references to the nineteenth-century Romantics
(Shelley and Byron among others). It was, the author claims —
though perhaps "erroneously," she cautions at the same time —
the "century-old enchantress" of the Romantic poem which had
come to life in her vision of Petersburg in 1913. But here her
Muse protests, denying all connection with "that English lady"
and saying she has no ancestors at all. In a formal sense, despite
the great number of literary echoes and allusions, this is indeed
true of "Poem without a Hero." It represents a conscious
attempt to go beyond the Romantic poem. For one thing,
Akhmatova believed that nobody could in any case successfully
follow in Pushkin's footsteps, and for another, her main pur-
pose was to recall an era in which there were no more heroes,
only pseudo-Romantic masqueraders; the hero-individualist
of the nineteenth century had come to the end of the road
and his epigones (unless, like Knyazev, they died young)
would be offered up wholesale to the Moloch of war and revo-
lution. The "real, not the calendar Twentieth Century" had
no need of heroes. Blok had demonstrated the impasse in his
work, particularly in "The Puppet Show" (1907), of which
there are echoes in "Poem without a Hero." The usual escape

was into irony, mummery, or blind devotion to an authoritarian creed.

Part Three (the Epilogue) is a majestic finale in which the theme of Part One is placed in the perspective of more recent tribulations and of Russia's struggle for survival in 1942: "All that was said in Part One / about love, betrayal and passion, / verse in free flight has shaken from its wings." She mentions the Terror and the concentration camps, identifying herself with the victims: "Behind the barbed wire / in the very heart of the dense taiga, / . . . my double goes to the interrogation." Alluding to her journey from Leningrad to Tashkent at the end of the terrible winter 1941–1942, she thinks in particular of her son, as the plane crosses the Urals: "And I saw that road, / over which so many went away, / over which they took my son." But at that moment, though the Soviet armies were everywhere in flight before the Germans, Russia was nevertheless gathering strength, getting ready to strike back along the same road. When Akhmatova finished the first draft of the "Poem" in Tashkent in August 1942, she did so in the somber conviction that if there was any hope of redemption, it could only be in Russia's victory over the evil threatening from without: "Away from what has turned to dust, / seized by fear of death, / yet sure of retribution's hour, / her tearless eyes cast down, / and wringing her hands, Russia / retreated there before me to the East. / But going out to meet herself, / unbowed into the carnage, / as though from a mirror before one's gaze, / like a hurricane from the Urals, from Altai, / true to her duty and young, / Russia marched forward to save Moscow."

Akhmatova regarded the "Poem without a Hero" as the crowning work of her life, a final distillation of memory, historical insight, and personal emotion into a poetic statement about the destiny of Russia. It thus ranks with Pushkin's "Bronze Horseman" and Alexander Blok's "The Twelve" (furthermore, Akhmatova succeeded where Blok failed in his unfinished "Retribution").

Some of Akhmatova's surviving contemporaries, as she herself mentioned in a letter to a friend in 1955, were upset by

Part One (which she evidently showed or read to some of them) because they felt she was "settling accounts" with the pre-Revolutionary decade and with people who could no longer defend themselves. She was aware that the "Poem" would be difficult, even incomprehensible, for anyone unfamiliar with certain "Petersburg events," but despite criticism on these grounds, she refused to make any concessions to the uninitiated. In the last years of her life, however, she divulged a few details in private conversation, and some of them were duly published — first by Kornei Chukovski in the literary journal *Moskva* in 1964, and then by E. Dobin in his important book *The Poetry of Anna Akhmatova* (Leningrad, 1968). Even with the clues given here the "Poem" remains difficult. As Akhmatova says, commenting on it herself in Part Two, it is "a box with a triple bottom." However many times one may read it, one can always discover new associations or suddenly see new perspectives, as though everything were indeed reflected in the mirrors that figure so prominently in the work. There are so many literary echoes and the texture is so dense, that it is rather like a palimpsest (as she herself indicated), even though one can point to no dominating influence in what is beyond doubt the most strikingly original long poem to be written in Russia since the Revolution. Akhmatova may "borrow" motifs, as a great composer might (the construction of the "Poem" is, indeed, like that of a symphony, with three distinct movements and recurring themes), but this is essential to the subtle patterning of a work which conveys the spirit of a whole age.

Mrs. Mandelstam has called the "Poem" a "recherche du temps perdu" and the comparison is apt. The genesis of the "Poem" is remarkably similar to that of Proust's novel (and likewise contains an actual description of the incident which released memory). Though the resemblance is surely fortuitous, Akhmatova was aware of Proust and must have read him: in her memoir of Modigliani, she mentions him together with Kafka and Joyce as one of the three pillars on which "the Twentieth Century now rests."

As mentioned above in the note to Poem 34, the nature of

time and identity is one of the major themes of the "Poem." It was something that much preoccupied Akhmatova in her last years — as is shown by the choice of title for her last volume, *The Flight of Time*. Others have pointed out that the apocalyptical "There shall be no more time" could have been one of the texts for the "Poem": in many places, here and elsewhere in her work, she seems to question the apparent immutability of the division of time into past, present, and future. This explains her concern (as also in Poem 33, "This Cruel Age Has Deflected Me . . .") with what might have been — with encounters that did not come about, with places she never visited. She is exercised by the irreversible "has-been-ness" of things, the irrevocability of what has happened. The mirror appears as a recurrent image in her poetry because it represents a "door" through which the past can reenter the present, or the present slip into the future.

The presence in the "Poem" of this element of speculation about time, not to mention the author's fascination with "doubles" and her deliberate blurring of fixed identity, has led some critics to see Akhmatova's later work as a regression from Acmeism back to Symbolism. In the second volume of her memoirs, Mrs. Mandelstam is inclined to believe there is truth in this, but the similarity is perhaps apparent rather than real. (What is more, Akhmatova herself once described her "Poem" as a "polemic" with Symbolism). Symbolism belonged to the era that preceded "the real, not the calendar Twentieth Century" and in its speculative aspect it was rooted, at the best, only in the imagination of its representatives. Akhmatova, on the other hand, was speaking not from imagination alone, but from the depth of unimaginable experience. The bemused uncertainty about time and identity which she communicates to the reader of "Poem without a Hero" is quite simply one of the everyday sensations born of such experience. Akhmatova joins Dostoyevski and Kafka in broadening the bounds of the contemporary imagination, helping it to take in the incredible realities of our epoch. What they only foreshadowed, she witnessed and described.

Page 147, "Here's one who comes as Faust": this and the following four lines contain references to stage performances or books which were popular in the few years before the Revolution. "John the Baptist" and "Salome's Dance" allude to Richard Strauss's opera (1905, based on Oscar Wilde's *Salome*) and a ballet by Fokine. "Dapertutto" was the commedia dell'arte pen name of Vsevolod Meyerhold which he used while editor of the literary and theatrical journal *Love of Three Apples* (1914–1916), to which both Akhmatova and Blok contributed. "Don Juan" (Meyerhold staged Molière's version of it in 1910) is a major theme in the "Poem." The epigraph to the whole work is from Da Ponte's libretto to Mozart's opera ("di rider finirai pria dell'aurora") and it is likely that the very concept of the "Poem" owes something to Pushkin's version of the legend, "The Stone Guest" (1830), which also opens with an epigraph from Mozart's *Don Giovanni*. There is a striking essay by Akhmatova on Pushkin's poem in which she points out its "confessional nature" (hence, she suggests, his unwillingness to publish it). He had chosen this theme of vengeance on the philanderer for its relevance to his own life, treating it in terms of sin and retribution. This essay of Akhmatova's concludes with a remark about Pushkin which applies in equal measure to herself: "Responding to 'every sound,' Pushkin absorbed the experience of the whole of his generation."

"The Nordic Glahn" is a character in Knut Hamsun's *Pan* (1894) who, like Knyazev, commits suicide.

"Goatlegged nymph": the reference is to Glebova-Sudeikina, the "heroine" of the "Poem." In late 1912 she danced in a ballet called *The Fauns* (music by Ilia Sats). There is a contemporary photograph showing Glebova-Sudeikina in the costume of a faun, with goat's horns.

Page 149, "they seek, cocoon of souls": The translation here takes a slight liberty with the original in order to render a phonetic detail by which Akhmatova set such store that she added a special note on it at the end of the "Poem": "The three 'k's betray the author's confusion."

"But look! there's one who hides his tail...": Read in

conjunction with further references in Part Two of the "Poem," this unflattering passage must be taken to apply to Mikhail Kuzmin.

"Till the Day of Judgment": the original refers to "the valley of Jehoshaphat," which Akhmatova annotates as "the presumed place of the Day of Judgment."

Page 151, "A sound of steps of those not here . . .": Akhmatova mentioned to several people in her later years that the image of the "visitor from the future" was inspired by an actual visitor from the West who came to see her not long after the war. It evidently struck her as providential and, given the circumstances of her life, was almost literally "from the future," as surely as the other "visitors" in the "Poem" were from the past. The extraordinary precision of detail shows how utterly real the visit was: in order to reach her apartment in a wing of the former Sheremetiyev palace, it would be necessary to turn left from a bridge over the Fontanka.

Page 151, "an extra shadow / without face or name / . . . you come in the gaudy stripes / of a painted milepost": this passage is about Blok. There is no obvious explanation of why Blok appears among the mummers dressed in this way. The striped milepost (*versta*) was a feature of the Russian landscape, and it has been suggested that there is here an association with Pushkin's poem "The Demons" (1830), in which at one moment, lost in a snowstorm, the poet mistakes a milepost for one of the demons that appear to be swirling around him. Since Blok's "demonic" nature is stressed here and elsewhere in "Poem without a Hero," not to mention that he was the author of a cycle of poems called "Snow Masks," Akhmatova may well have had in mind Pushkin's demon appearing as a milepost through the blizzard.

Page 151, "the Mamre oak": See Genesis xiv: 13, 24, etc.

Page 155, "I am ready for death": In her memoir on Mandelstam, Akhmatova recalls that as she was walking with him along a Moscow street one day in February 1934 (about three months before his arrest), he said these words to her. The fact that she puts them in the mouth of Knyazev in "Poem without a Hero" is a good example of the deliberate blurring of

172

identity mentioned earlier. Similarly, the image of Glebova-Sudeikina to some extent merges with her own, and with that of Salome Andronnikova (the very same words — "elegant and tall" — are used of Glebova-Sudeikina in "Poem without a Hero" as of Salome Andronnikova in "In 1940").

Page 155, "or is someone really standing there again / between the stove and cupboard?": B. A. Filippov has pointed out that these lines are clearly inspired by the description of Kirillov in Dostoyevski's *Possessed*, after he had hanged himself: "In the corner formed by the wall and the cupboard, Kirillov was standing — and standing in a terribly strange manner."